EXPLORE MEMPHIS!
A GUIDE FOR FAMILY ACTIVITIES

DEBBIE MONROE • MARCI SWEENEY

Illustrations by Jill Dubin

Buckhead Press

1431 Woodmont Lane, Suite 101
Atlanta, Georgia 30318
(404) 350-9355

Edited by PATTI SEIKUS
Illustrations by JILL DUBIN
Typography by STAN HIXON & PATTI SEIKUS

ISBN 0-9628349-1-2

We dedicate this book to the five people who provided the patience, cooperation, and love necessary to make its creation possible. They are the same five people who supply the focus for all the explorations and celebrations in our lives: Mitchell Sweeney, Sally Monroe, Graham Sweeney, Jay Sweeney, and John Monroe.

D.M. and M.S.

ACKNOWLEDGMENTS

Fearful of likely omissions of obvious names, we, nevertheless, bravely venture forth to list friends and family members without whose support we could not have completed this book. Their specific acts of guidance and assistance and encouragement directly contributed to the creation of *Explore Memphis!*. With heartfelt gratitude, we acknowledge the splendid gifts of time, experience, wisdom, and labor of the following wonderful explorers:

Marilou Awiakta
Pan Awsumb
Brin and Dale Baucum
Gwen Blackburn
Ione and Roy Bruce
Marie Brown
Jack Childers
Renee Cooley
Peggy and Steve Copen
Carol Ekstrom
Geri Forehand
John Glenzer
March and Mitch Hall
Peggy Purifoy
Ronna Rachelson
Stephanie Rodda
Judith Sigsbee
Ginger and Charlie Taylor
Sharon Taylor
Nancy Thompson
Jackie Vannice
Phil Waldon
Irene Warner

If we forgot you, please accept our deepest apologies. (To be perfectly honest, we approached this task with more apprehension than the writing of the book itself.)

TABLE OF CONTENTS

Memphis Parent, a bimonthly newspaper for today's active families, is published by the Metropolitan Inter-Faith Association (MIFA) as part of its youth services. Created in 1968 as a non-profit human service agency, MIFA has built a credible reputation by combining income from many sources, both public and private, to provide life's basic necessities for children and adults in crisis. MIFA also seeks to involve the entire Memphis community in its outreach efforts.

As part of MIFA's mission, *Memphis Parent* seeks to strengthen families from all walks of life and to help young people become positive, productive citizens. By providing information on parent/child issues, family activities and other timely topics, *Memphis Parent* serves as a valuable resource to families.

Straight To The Heart

1. Introduction

At least once or twice a year each of our families decides to take a trip out of town. Sometimes there is a work-related reason for the trip; other times we choose a vacation spot for one special feature we've heard about. But whether our choice of trip destination is well thought out or externally imposed or fairly random, we want to learn as much as possible about it before ever beginning our journey. The first thing we do when we find out we'll be visiting another city is to rush to the public library and bookstores to see what there is to do and see in the place where we'll be vacationing. After all, we don't want to waste any of our precious sightseeing time deciding what to do once we get there.

Out of curiosity one day, we decided to see what guidelines were available to tourists visiting Memphis. We couldn't find any Memphis guidebooks for families. Then, as we visited other cities, we searched their bookstores for Memphis information — still with little success.

How could this be? After all, Memphis is one of the 20 largest cities in the United States. A major transportation hub, Memphis is arguably the pork barbecue capital of the world; a focal point for the world's cotton, soybean, and hardwood markets; a cultural center for the Mid-South; and a top tourist destination. There is no doubt that Memphis deserves a reliable, convenient, easy-to-read compilation of major attractions, sports events, performances, and other recreational activities that would be appealing to families with children — preschoolers to teens. (Although our guide is intentionally directed toward the needs of the traditional family, we believe it will also prove to be a useful tool for single adults, teachers, day care directors, and any others who are looking for ways to locate and explore the many worthwhile places to spend leisure time in and around Memphis.)

What started out as an intention to list and describe all the wonderful, entertaining, and naturally familiar spots in Memphis turned out to be an enterprise that surprised and delighted us. We thought we knew every place there was to go, but of course good research principles demanded that we not only know about the attractions, but also visit the ones that had somehow previously escaped our attention.

In this process we discovered enchanting out-of-the-way places we had never gotten around to visiting firsthand. When word of our project spread to our friends and acquaintances, we learned of even more fascinating well-kept secrets. Memphis turned into a tourists' haven for us — long-time Memphians.

Let us warn you that you might consider some of our suggestions a bit unconventional. Given a choice between a high-tech, neon-flashing ride at an amusement park and the worm-eaten timbers of an old barn, chances are pretty slim that we would opt for the bright lights. Many places that were not originally designed as tourist attractions have become cherished over the years for their stumbled-upon entertainment value. It is the bird dog museum or riverboat ride, not the shopping mall or miniature golf course, that gives a place its own special flavor.

However, we realize that tastes vary, and we enjoy a couple of rounds on the putt-putt course as much as the next family, so we have done our best to provide you with a smattering of all types of entertainment opportunities — from the ultra-modern, squeaky-clean attraction to the time-tested classic to the off-the-beaten-path discovery. We hope that all our selections possess a genuine intrinsic value to keep your sense of adventure stirred up and begging for more.

You are sure to find something new and exciting within these pages. We hope that you have as much fun exploring your new territories as we have had finding them for you.

Note that all phone numbers in this book, unless otherwise indicated, are prefixed by the 901 Memphis area code.

2. Places to Go

No bones about it: these are the places in and near Memphis that you MUST visit! You might get away with skipping a handful, but any self-respecting family will face unbearable ridicule if is members are not somewhat conversant with the majority of the listings in Chapter 2.

Now that we've given you a practical rationale — license, if you will — to go out and have fun, do just that!

If there is an attraction you expect but fail to find here, chances are you'll find it in Chapter 3, which also lists popular, but for the most part, smaller attractions.

For your convenience, the listings in Chapter 2 are alphabetized. Look for the symbols below to help you locate at a glance the particular brand of fun you're seeking.

 NATURE

 SCIENCE

 UNIQUE ATTRACTION

 HISTORY AND GOVERNMENT

 PERFORMING ARTS

 FINE ARTS

ADVENTURE RIVER WATER PARK

6880 Whitten Bend Cove
Memphis, Tennessee 38133 • 382-9283

Adventure River Water Park offers 25 acres of exciting activities specially designed for fun seekers of all ages. The park features a 21,000-square-foot wave pool, a lazy river, two speed slides, three coiled body slides, two tube slides, and a children's activity pool and play area. A highly trained aquatic staff is available at all attractions.

Although some attractions have height and weight requirements, there is something for everyone to enjoy. Ample lounge chairs afford relaxation for those wishing to kick back and stay cool. Admission to the park includes inner tube usage and life jackets if desired. Free showers are also available.

Group outing specialists are on staff to help plan birthday parties, picnics, family reunions, and other group gatherings. A complete catering menu for 30 or more guests is available for such events. (Call 382-WAVE for information.)

- Brochure available.

- Free tours are available during operating hours.

- Free parking.

- Special events, such as Mom's Monday and Christian Family Music Night, are planned throughout the summer. Call for details.

- Concession areas are located throughout the park. Picnic baskets and coolers are permitted in the picnic area only.

- The park is a multi-service facility, complete with a gift shop, an arcade, changing areas, lockers, volleyball courts, and a softball field.

- Appropriate swim attire is required. No cutoffs allowed. No bottles or alcoholic beverages allowed.

- Handicapped accessibility to the park itself, the gift shop, and rest rooms. The wave pool and lazy river are also handicapped accessible.

- Rest rooms, diaper changing areas, and water fountains are available throughout the park.

Hours: Open weekends in May 10 a.m.-6 p.m., Memorial Day weekend 10 a.m.-8 p.m., June through most of August 10 a.m.-8 p.m., end of August 11 a.m.-6 p.m., Labor Day weekend 10 a.m.-8 p.m. Closed the remainder of the year. (Hours, dates, and rates subject to change without advance notice. Call ahead to confirm schedule and fees.)

Admission: Ages 3 and under, free; 4-59, $12.99; 60 and above, $6.99. Season passes and group rates available.

Directions: Exit #14 off I-40 east, between Germantown Road and Sycamore View exits.

AGRICENTER INTERNATIONAL

7777 Walnut Grove Road
Memphis, Tennessee 38120 • 757-7777

The identity of Memphis, Tennessee, is deeply rooted in the agriculture industry. Located in the fertile region of the southern United States and well-placed as a central distribution point for agricultural and other products, Memphis is the natural home of Agricenter International, an incredible resource for farmers, as well as any adults and children interested in the dynamic and varied world of food production. Opened in 1986, Agricenter bills itself as an agri-technology facility.

The focal point of the Agricenter is the Exhibition Pavilion, which contains 140,000 square feet of exhibit areas and meeting rooms. There are permanent and temporary displays of all sorts of agricultural products, from chemicals to massive machinery. Major shows of interest to families with limited understanding of agriculture are the Festival of Trees in December; the Farm, Home, and Garden Show in March; and the Farm, Home, and the Energy Show in October.

The facility also houses the National Weather Service, which provides continuous broadcasts of weather conditions and forecasts for the three-state area of Tennessee, Arkansas, and Mississippi. Tours are available through arrangement by calling 757-6400.

Another unique feature of the Agricenter is its 52-acre Aquaculture Center. Here catfish, crawfish, tilapia, and bass farming can be viewed. Call 755-2782 for details.

Hydroponic gardening (cucumbers and tomatoes) takes place in greenhouses at the Agricenter. Tours are available. Call 753-2714 for more information.

Public fishing at the Agricenter's lake is available. The fee is $1 per person (age 10 and up) and $1.75 per pound of catfish. (Children 9 and under can fish for free.) Call 755-9255 for details.

A recommended family activity is driving through the land resource itself. Testing plots where such crops as cotton, corn, wheat, and sorghum are grown provide an introduction to the world of agriculture. Your family might be fortunate enough to be on hand when gigantic machines are tilling the soil or harvesting the crops or when the irrigation system is in full operation.

- Brochures and newsletters are available in the Exhibition Pavilion.

- Guided tours of Agricenter Pavilion can be arranged for school groups, clubs, etc. by calling 757-7777 about two weeks in advance. The tours are set up for Tuesday, Wednesday, and Thursday mornings from 10 to 11 a.m.

- The Agricenter's "break room," which is open to the public, offers sandwich machines and snack machines. Soda machines are located throughout the building. Although there are no picnic tables, picnicking on the grounds is allowed.

- Full accessibility to the handicapped.

- Rest rooms and water fountains are available.

Hours: Monday through Friday, 8 a.m.-4:30 p.m., and on some weekends, depending on special shows and events.

Admission: Admission to the Agricenter is free unless there is a special event or show which requires admission. Prices would vary with the particular event. Call ahead.

Directions: From I-40 take the Walnut Grove East exit. The Agricenter is located on the right-hand side of Walnut Grove, about five or six minutes away from I-40 (just before Germantown Parkway).

AUDUBON PARK

4145 Southern
Memphis, Tennessee 38119

Memphis has a wealth of parks located within the city's boundaries. One of the larger, more diverse facilities is the 373-acre Audubon Park situated in the eastern part of the city.

Major attractions finding their home in Audubon are Memphis Botanic Garden (see listing in this chapter) and Leftwich Tennis Center, which includes both indoor and outdoor courts. A great deal of the park comprises the 18-hole Audubon Public Golf Course. The clubhouse, with carts available, is located near the southwest corner of the park. Although reservations are needed for the tennis courts at the Leftwich Center (call 685-7907), there are outdoor courts near the golf clubhouse that are free and available on a first-come, first-served basis.

In the northeast corner of the park several picnic tables, complete with stone grills, are waiting for _al fresco_ dining groups. A playground, covered pavilion, and basketball court complete the amenities.

If you enter the park at the Perkins Road (east) side, you will find a small lake equipped with a fishing pier and ducks to feed. Fishing is permitted for anyone under 16 or over 65 years of age (no charge or license required). A covered pavilion with rest rooms is nearby, along with plenty of picnic tables. Athletic fields and open areas are also available.

- Parking is available throughout the park.

- Special events are scheduled during the year, both in the botanic garden and in the rest of the park. The Pink Palace Crafts Fair, an annual event taking place the first weekend in October, is a popular regional festival with fine crafts, food, and entertainment for the entire family.

- Rest rooms and water fountains can be found at covered pavilions.

Hours: Open 6 a.m.-midnight.

Admission: FREE.

Directions: Located in east Memphis near Memphis State University, Audubon Park is bordered on the north by Southern Avenue, the east by Perkins, the south by Park Avenue, and the west by Goodlett.

CENTER FOR SOUTHERN FOLKLORE

152 Beale Street
Memphis, Tennessee 38103 • 525-3655

Founded in 1972, the Center for Southern Folklore moved in 1989 from an old house on Peabody to its present Beale Street location. The street that fanned the embers of the developing blues music tradition in the early part of the 20th century is an appropriate home for this repository of memorabilia from the rich musical history of the Mid-South. Priceless resources generated by and preserved by the Center for Southern Folklore include video and audio tape recordings of area musicians, crafts makers, and storytellers. The films can be viewed at the center for $1.50 per person per film.

Other features of the Center for Southern Folklore are archives, books, and artifacts relating to the South, as well as an outdoor exhibit on Beale Street in the form of markers along the street detailing the area's rich musical history. Changing exhibits might present quilts, jewelry, baskets, carvings, dolls, or any number of southern treats.

Documenting and presenting the traditions and people of the South, the Center for Southern Folklore provides a good foundation for adults or children interested in the heritage of this region and serves as a valuable educational and research guide.

- Brochures are available.

- Beale Street Walking Tours are conducted for a minimum of five people. Fees are $4.50 for adults; $3.50 for senior citizens and children; and $2 for children under 12. Call for appointments.

- Free parking is available in lots behind the buildings on the opposite (south) side of Beale.

- The gift shop features uniquely southern gift items.

- Popular annual events sponsored by the Center for Southern Folklore include the Mid-South Music and Heritage Festival (second weekend in July), the Annual Folk Art and Craft Show (November-February), and the special exhibit for Black History Month (February).

- Handicapped accessibility is provided by an elevator to the fourth-floor entrance and third-floor exit of the center.

- Rest rooms and water fountain available.

Hours: Monday-Saturday, 9 a.m.-5:30 p.m.; Sunday,1-5:30 p.m.

Admission: $2 Adults; $1 12 and under; $1 Senior adults

Directions: In downtown Memphis, between Second and Third Streets on Beale.

THE CHILDREN'S MUSEUM OF MEMPHIS

2525 Central Avenue
Memphis, Tennessee 38104 • 458-2678

With the welcoming motto "Please Touch!", The Children's Museum of Memphis invites even the youngest visitors to learn by doing, imagining, making choices, and creating. Located in an attractively preserved historic building that once was home to the Tennessee National Guard, The Children's Museum opened its doors in 1990 to a first-year attendance of over 200,000.

Permanent exhibits contained in an innovative 12,000-square-foot environment called CityScape include child-sized versions of the major components of a metropolitan area. Some favorite make-believe activities are shopping for groceries, banking, romping in the toddler "play park," and hopping aboard the fire engine in full fire fighter costume. Children can crawl through a manhole or climb a skyscraper, staff a 911 center, or drive a car.

In addition to its permanent exhibits and excellent changing exhibits, The Children's Museum offers numerous special programs. **Time Out for Tots** is a Thursday-morning program designed for children under 5 who pay a fee of $2-$3 per session (advance registration required). Previous topics include Johnny Appleseed Surprise, Mickey Mouse's Birthday

Party, and Teddies and Tea. **Wonderful Wednesdays** (4 p.m. programs) are open to all (free with regular admission). Topics revolve around recycling fun, such as a peace collage, goblins from garbage, and cartoon costumes. **Young Chefs**, a 10 a.m.-noon Saturday morning workshop, provides hands-on cooking experience for varying age groups. Previous courses include Pizza Power, Hershey Heaven, and Banana Bop and Super Sundaes (registration and fee of $12-$15 required). Other workshops, holiday events, and day camps take place at The Children's Museum. Watch the newspaper for special listings or call for a list of current activities.

- Brochures are available at the museum, along with a monthly calendar of events and *Sparks*, the museum's quarterly newsletter.

- Reservations are always required for group visits. Call 458-2678. Group rates available.

- Free parking on the lot, with plenty of room for buses and vans.

- No food, drink, or smoking in the museum. All children must be accompanied by an adult.

- Be sure to visit the wonderful gift shop stocked with creative and educational treasures for children and their parents. The revenue from the shop is used to support the museum's educational programs, exhibits, and general operating costs.

- Suggested activities are Andy Ambulance (every Friday at 4 p.m.) and Hello Stuffee demonstration (Tuesdays and Sundays at 4 p.m.).

- The museum's Van Vleet changing exhibit area offers new exhibits all the time. Special events are scheduled around holidays.

- Picnic tables are located on the front lawn of the museum.

- The museum is handicapped accessible.

- Rest rooms and a diaper changing area are located in the museum. A water fountain is available.

Hours: Tuesday-Saturday, 10 a.m.-5 p.m.; Sunday, 1-5 p.m. Closed Mondays, some holidays, and days of some Memphis State University home football games.

Admission: Children 1-12 and senior citizens (62+), $3; other adults and teens, $4. Various membership levels (family $45 per year) offer free admission, quarterly newsletter, monthly calendar, discounts, advance notice of programs and events, and birthday party rental privileges.

Directions: Located at the corner of Central Avenue and Hollywood on the grounds of the Liberty Bowl Stadium at the Mid-South Fairgrounds.

CHUCALISSA ARCHAEOLOGICAL MUSEUM

1987 Indian Village Drive
Memphis, Tennessee 38109 • 785-3160

Chucalissa, which meant "abandoned house" to the Mississippian Indians who once inhabited this site, is an apt name for this museum. The Native Americans who lived here around the 15th century have long-since "abandoned the house" (this is NOT a reservation or living Indian village), but the village has been partially reconstructed on the actual site. The realistic setting includes thatched huts, mounds, and a plaza area.

The charms of Chucalissa, combined with children's fascination with the cultures of the Native Americans, attract numerous groups from schools throughout the Mid-South. Elementary-aged children enjoy going into the thatched huts and climbing atop the mounds. Exhibits covering the prehistory of the area and southeastern Indian culture, along with many interesting artifacts and simulated living situations, merit the attention of children, as well as their parents.

Permanent exhibits include methods of archaeology, preserved archaeological trench excavation, and reconstructed houses. Affiliation with Memphis State University's Department of Anthropology helps ensure the quality of the offerings at Chucalissa.

The visit to Chucalissa includes a 15-minute introductory slide program, the museum hall, and the outside area. Visitors self-guide through the facilities. With advance reservations for groups of 10 or more, guided tours by Choctaw Indian staff members (enhanced by craft demonstrations) are available.

Previous readings about Native Americans can increase the pleasure of the Chucalissa experience. (Call the museum ahead of time for suggestions.)

- Brochures are available.

- Plenty of free parking is available in the parking lot. There is room for buses and vans.

- Adults are responsible for control of groups. The basic park adage applies: "Take nothing but pictures; leave nothing but footprints."

- There is a gift shop, which includes some Native American crafts.

- The Choctaw Indian Heritage Festival takes place on the first weekend of August. Call the museum for other highlights of the year.

- Vending machines in the museum provide soft drinks and snacks. Picnic tables are located near the parking lot. T.O. Fuller State Park, on the adjacent grounds, offers playground equipment, camping, and picnic shelters.

- The museum and village area are accessible to wheelchairs, but there is no access to the top of the mounds.

- There are rest rooms and water fountains.

Hours: Tuesday-Saturday, 9 a.m.-5 p.m.; Sunday, 1-5 p.m.; closed Mondays (no admission to village area after 4:30 p.m.)

Admission: Adults 12-59, $3; children 4-11, $1.50; senior citizens (60+), $1.50. Discount for groups of 10 or more with advance reservations.

Directions: From I-240 take I-55 N to Third Street exit. Follow Third Street south to third stoplight (Mitchell Road); turn right. Drive about five miles and follow the signs after reaching T.O. Fuller State Park.

CITY HALL

125 N. Mid-America Mall
Memphis, Tennessee

This modern seat of government houses the mayor's office, the City Council chambers, and other offices conducting business for the city of Memphis.

A visit to City Hall is a good time to talk about the way our government works. Children who are particularly interested in the structure and locale of city government might enjoy visits to the nearby centers for the Shelby County, Tennessee, and United States local affairs. (City Hall, the Clifford Davis Federal Building, the Tennessee State Office Building, and the Shelby County Building form a semi-circle around the north end of Mid-America Mall at Poplar Avenue.)

The Hall of Mayors lining the north portion of the walls of City Hall at the entrance level lobby is a good place to begin the visit. Another interesting historical tidbit on display is a piece of a historical cannon that fired the first salute to the new United States flag in 1776. The lobby also features changing exhibits that focus on local culture. Outside the north entrance to the building, look for the Liberty Bowl bell and the parade of patriotic flags.

- An information center is located in the lobby.

- Parking is available in the Mud Island pay lot directly across Front Street.

- Vending machines are available at the entrance level. Quick hot foods are available at Penny's Snack Bar on level 1B. Excellent luncheon establishments are situated south on Mid-America Mall and nearby Downtown streets.

- Handicapped accessible.

- Rest rooms and water fountain available.

Hours: Monday-Friday business hours.

Admission: FREE.

Directions: West on Poplar Avenue, left on Front Street; City Hall is at the heart of downtown Memphis.

CORDOVA CELLARS

9050 Macon Road
Cordova, Tennessee 38018 • 754-3442

Cordova Cellars is a family-owned and -operated estate winery located just northeast of Memphis in Cordova, Tennessee. The three-story brick and redwood winery, designed to resemble a traditional cross-shaped barn, sits alongside the 4 1/2 acres of vines on lushly landscaped grounds with a picnic area for use by visitors.

Planted in 1987, the commercial vineyard consists of varieties of Chardonnay and Vidal Blanc, which have been found to be two of the most promising varieties for growing in Tennessee. The winery expects to plant an additional two to three acres in the near future.

A tour of the winery includes a visit to the actual production room with an informative description of the process of wine-making. From the crusher and on to the press, each step is displayed and explained. Huge tanks and barrels, fermenting a variety of wines, line the room. A hand-bottling demonstration concludes the tour of the winery, after which visitors may browse the gift shop and taste the wines if desired. Everyone is encouraged to walk through the vineyards in self-paced fashion at this point.

The winery often is host to art exhibits, outdoor lawn concerts, wine appreciation classes, and tastings. The meeting room on the main level is available to various groups (for a fee) for meetings, luncheons, seminars, etc.

- Brochures available.

- Drop-in tours available. Group reservations are requested.

- The gift shop sells wine and wine-related gifts (T-shirts, books, etc.).

- Harvest of the grapes usually occurs in August. Volunteers are often recruited to assist in the harvest. Call ahead for information.

- The winery is handicapped accessible.

- Rest rooms and water are available.

Hours: Tuesday-Saturday, 10 a.m.-5 p.m.; Sunday, 1-5 p.m. Abbreviated hours at some times. Call ahead for holiday and winter (January and February) schedules.

Admission: FREE.

Directions: Drive east out of Memphis on Walnut Grove Road. Turn left (north) on Germantown Parkway. Turn right onto Macon Road. Drive through the pastoral setting of Cordova; signs will be posted for Cordova Cellars on the left.

THE DIXON GALLERY AND GARDENS

4339 Park Avenue
Memphis, Tennessee 38117 • 761-5250

This specialized fine arts museum and gardens opened in 1976 and was the bequest of the late Margaret and Hugo Dixon, philanthropists and cultural leaders in Memphis. The Dixons left their home, gardens, and art collections for the education and enrichment of the community.

The Dixon Gallery has one of the South's finest collections of paintings by impressionists and post-impressionists. The former residence is furnished with porcelain, sculpture and 18th-century furniture acquired by Mr. and Mrs. Dixon.

Landscaped in the manner of an English park, the 17-acre gardens surrounding the Gallery are a delight to children. Complete with open vistas and a series of formal and informal gardens, the grounds are an oasis in an urban setting during all seasons.

In addition to the Gallery's permanent exhibit, special exhibits on loan from other institutions change regularly. Some past exhibits of particular interest to children include the Toulouse Lautrec collection and the American West, which depicts legendary artists of the frontier.

- Brochures are available in the main lobby entrance.

- Organized groups may arrange docent-guided gallery and garden tours by appointment. Call 761-5250 for reservations and information.

- No cameras with flash are allowed. Visitors should be quiet in the Gallery.

- Holiday workshops for children, along with performing arts programs and lectures, are offered regularly.

- There is a small gift shop.

- There is direct handicapped access to the Gallery and limited access to the Gardens.

- Rest rooms and water fountains are available.

Hours: Tuesday-Saturday, 10 a.m.-5 p.m.; Sunday 1-5 p.m. Closed Mondays and holidays.

Admission: Adults, $3.50; students and senior citizens, $2.50; children under 12, $1; children under 4, free. Tuesdays are FREE.

Directions: The Gallery and Gardens are located in East Memphis on the south side of Park Avenue between Getwell and Perkins Avenues.

DOWNTOWN PARK TOUR

An extraordinary feature of Memphis, Tennessee, is its park system. Boasting of Audubon and Overton Parks and a variety of wonderful large and small facilities in residential and suburban areas, Memphis also enjoys an abundance of lushly wooded, well-maintained parks situated right in the heart of the Downtown business district. Choose any or all of the parks we have featured here in the Downtown park tour, or venture out on a park expedition of your own. (As in any setting that comprises lots of open and secluded spaces that are unsupervised, we recommend that you practice basic safety rules of avoiding dark or isolated spots and touring with companions.)

Begin your tour at **Court Square,** which is bounded by N. Court, Mid-America Mall, S. Court, and Second Streets. The land for this lovely square oasis (2.2 acres) in an urban setting was donated to the city of Memphis in 1819 and turned into Court Square in 1829. Points of particular interest include the Hebe Fountain, erected in 1876 and rumored to be one of only a handful of its kind in the world; the numerous historical markers and monuments; the 1986 time capsule; and the garfish-motif park benches. The squirrels and pigeons in this park are practically on a first-name basis with the Downtown workers who like to steal away from their offices during lunch break. If you would like to make the animals' acquaintance, too, a bag of peanuts is all you need by way of introduction. The Peanut Shoppe is just a block-and-a-half away (south to 24 S. Main). Hawking both pigeon food and people food (candies, nuts, popcorn) is the mechanized Peanut Man with his monocle and cane tapping away at a dime on the window. The old peanut roasters provide both visual and olfactory delights. (Drinking fountains are built into the Hebe Fountain at Court Square, but rest room facilities are usually locked.)

One block west of Court Square (toward the river at Jefferson and Riverside) is **Confederate Park**, also laid out in 1829. Adorned by a statue of Jefferson Davis and other monuments, the 2.6-acre park also contains a large Confederate plaque on the southwest corner detailing the history of the Memphis Confederacy. The bluff edge on the west overlooks Jefferson Davis Park, the Wolf River Harbor, Mud Island, the Mississippi River, and the Arkansas shoreline. Also along the western section of the park are interesting 20th-century artillery pieces.

Descending the bluff via steps at the southwest corner of Confederate Park, you will come upon **Jefferson Davis Park** after crossing Riverside Drive. Jefferson Davis Park, with its 2.4 acres established in 1930, continues with the garfish benches found in Court Square. Offering a view from the same direction, but at a lower altitude than Confederate Park, Jefferson Davis Park gives visitors a closer perspective on Mud Island, but the island blocks much of the river view seen from above.

The **River Promenade** (designed by architects March and Mitch Hall, who also were responsible for the renovation of Court Square and Jefferson Davis Park) can be found at the southeast corner of Jefferson Davis Park. Leading north to The Pyramid or south over the cobblestones to **Tom Lee Park,** the riverwalk is a symbol of Memphians' reverence for park preservation and desire for easy access to the parks. With its wide open spaces and close proximity to the Mississippi River, Tom Lee Park (eight acres set aside in 1914) is a popular spot for picnicking, tossing balls, flying kites, or lying on quilts and watching barges float by on the river.

GRACELAND

3764 Elvis Presley Boulevard
Memphis, Tennessee 38186 • 332-3322

Graceland Mansion is situated on 13.8 acres in the south Memphis suburb of Whitehaven. Built as a country home in 1939, the property was purchased by Elvis Presley, the internationally renowned singer (with sales of over one billion records) and film star (31 feature films), in 1957 for about $100,000. Since its opening to the public in 1982, Graceland has become one of the most recognized estates and one of the most popular memorial museums in the nation.

Ninety-minute tours of 16-18 persons start every several minutes from Graceland Plaza across the street from the home's lawn. The plaza area includes the ticket pavilion, gift shops, restaurants, the Elvis Presley Automobile Museum, Elvis's jets (the Lisa Marie and Jetstar) and tour bus, and a parking lot.

Shuttle buses carry visitors from the plaza to the mansion's front steps. Inside, guides tell the stories of each room, relate anecdotes about Elvis, and answer questions. Highlights include the TV Room, the Jungle Room, and the Trophy Room, which holds Elvis's gold-record collection and many costumes he wore. There is a pause at the Meditation Garden, where Elvis, his parents, and his grandmother are buried.

Thousands of visitors from all over the world come each year to visit Graceland. Quite different from the typical restored-home tour, this one is a must for the numerous fans of Elvis Presley and the rock 'n roll music he created.

•   All the amenities of a popular tourist attraction: brochures, rest rooms, water fountains, restaurants, and gift shops can be found in Graceland Plaza, the reception area across the street from Graceland Mansion.

- There is a fee for parking in the Graceland Plaza lot. Limited free parking is available in gift shop lots farther north on Elvis Presley Boulevard.

- Many special events commemorating Elvis's birthdate (January 8, 1935) and the date of his death (August 16, 1977) attract busloads of fan clubs and individual visitors at these times each year. Special Christmas decorations make Graceland particularly appealing during December also.

- Tours of the mansion are guided and take place on a timed schedule. Other attraction tours are self-paced.

- Graceland is partially accessible to the handicapped. (Ask about the Combo #2 ticket, which includes all attractions except the tour bus and airplanes. Wheelchairs may be borrowed, with certain restrictions. Call Graceland Guest Services for more details.) Ample handicapped parking spaces are provided.

Hours: March-October, daily; November-February, every day except Tuesday. Closed major winter holidays. Memorial Day-Labor Day tours begin regularly from 8 a.m. till 6 p.m.; remainder of the year tours begin regularly from 9 a.m. till 5 p.m.

Admission: Adults, $7.95; children 4-12, $4.75; children under 4, free. Separate fees are charged for the additional attractions. Combination tickets, including the mansion, the planes, the tour bus, the "Elvis-Up-Close" Museum, the automobile museum, and a 20-minute film can be purchased for $15.95 for adults and $10.95 for children.

Directions: Approximately 10 miles from downtown Memphis. Drive I-55 South to Exit 5B (Hwy. 51 S., AKA Elvis Presley Boulevard), and drive one mile south to Graceland. Parking is on the west side only of Elvis Presley Boulevard.

HISTORIC BEALE STREET

Beale Street Management
168 Beale Street
Memphis, Tennessee 38103 • 526-0110

Beale Street, Memphis, Tennessee, is the spot about which W.C. Handy, Father of the Blues, proclaimed, "I'd rather be here than any place I know." Designated a historic landmark by the National Register, the two blocks of Beale between Second and Fourth are the center of the five-block district stretching to The Orpheum at Beale and Front.

Restaurants, gift shops, and nightclubs abound. Historic markers are strategically placed to tell Beale Street's colorful story. The "Walk of Fame," which features brass musical notes inlaid in the sidewalk, memorializes such Memphis music greats as Alberta Hunter, Furry Lewis, B.B. King, the Newborn Family, and others who helped to create the unique character of the district.

Modern-day Beale Street supports and encourages an ongoing musical tradition with a multitude of events, such as the Memphis Music Festivals (spring and fall), the Beale Street Music Festival, the Traditional Jazz Festival, and Blues Week. The tradition of southern cooking, from barbecue to catfish, lives on, too, at Beale Street.

Although the nighttime activities on Beale are geared to adults, the daytime street is a great place for a family to shop in absolutely one-of-a-kind shops or to stroll while appreciating the rich history permeating the district. Don't miss the W.C. Handy and Elvis Presley statues! (For additional attractions on Beale street, see listings in this chapter for A. Schwab, Center for Southern Folklore, Memphis Police Museum, and The Orpheum.)

- An array of brochures and other helpful information is available at the Visitor Information Center, 340 Beale Street.

- Other nearby attractions include Memphis Music and Blues Museum and The Peabody (check listings in this chapter).

- Ample free parking is available in the lots behind the buildings on the south side of Beale.

- Most locations are handicapped accessible.

Hours: Nighttime activities directed toward adult entertainment. Daytime activities suitable for families. Check individual attractions for hours of operation.

Admission: No admission fee to the historic district.

Directions: From east Memphis, follow Union Avenue west. Turn left at Fourth Street and right on Beale. Beale Street lies in downtown Memphis, one block from The Peabody; one mile from Mud Island, the Memphis Convention Center, and Crowne Plaza.

LAUREL HILL VINEYARD

1370 Madison Avenue
Memphis, Tennessee 38104 • 725-9128

Laurel Hill Vineyard is a small estate winery in the Midtown area of Memphis. Although located on a major Memphis street, the winery is often overlooked. The building is a 1918 Sears and Roebuck "made-to-order" house. An effort is being made to preserve the exterior's original appearance in spite of modifications necessitated by such requirements as handicapped accessibility.

A tour of the winery includes an educational slide presentation showing the vineyard from the time it is planted and pruned through the growing season to the harvest and bottling. Questions are encouraged. All wines may be sampled or purchased.

Laurel Hill's own vineyards are located approximately 175 miles from Memphis on the southwest corner of the Cumberland Plateau.

- Brochures are available.

- Tours take place on a drop-in basis. Groups of 40 or more need to make a reservation.

- A selection of wine-related gifts, souvenirs, and books is available at the gift shop.

- Parking lot is located at the rear of the building (free).

- Periodic wine appreciation classes and wine tastings are available. Call for schedule.

- Handicapped accessible.

- Rest rooms are available. Water available on request.

Hours: Monday-Friday, 10 a.m.-12:30 p.m., 1:30-5:30 p.m. Also open Saturday 10 a.m.-2 p.m. during November and December.

Admission: FREE.

Directions: The winery is on the north side of Madison, just east of Cleveland Street and is easily reached from the western segment of I-240 connecting I-40 and I-55.

LIBERTYLAND

Mid-South Fairgrounds
Early Maxwell Boulevard
Memphis, Tennessee 38104 • 274-1776

Are you ready for fun and excitement? Libertyland, which opened on July 4, 1976 (the 200th birthday of the United States), is a historical, educational, and recreational amusement park that offers fun for the entire family, revolving around its patriotic theme.

The park's beautifully landscaped grounds are filled with live shows featuring pop and country music, a unique children's theatre, a special playground for children, thrill rides, delicious foods, games, quaint shops, and special events.

Give yourself a lift on the Whirl-a-Wheel (the Ferris wheel with a patriotic flair), the Zippin Pippin (the oldest operating wooden roller coaster in North America), or the Grand Carousel. (Built in 1909 by William H. Dentzel of the famed Dentzel Carousel Company, it is made up of 48 completely restored, hand-carved wooden horses. This ride is listed with the National Register of Historic Places.)

At Kid's Korner and Tom Sawyer's Island, located inside the park, the sized-down rides are suited for the smallest youngsters.

Give your taste buds a treat too. Pronto Pups, Italian sausage, funnel cakes, cotton candy, frosted fruit drinks, and more are available as you stroll through the park. Southern cookin' or American classic foods can be enjoyed at sit-down restaurants.

• Brochures and maps of the park are available.

- Parking is available on the grounds. There is no fee except during special events such as the Mid-South Fair. Additional parking is available along the bordering streets.

- Picnic areas are located throughout the park.

- Several unique gift shops are located within the park.

- Special facilities and catering are available for groups.

- Libertyland, at various times throughout the year, hosts such special events as the Mid-South Fair (September), the Muscular Dystrophy Telethon (Labor Day), Memphis in May activities, the Children's International Festival, and a big Fourth of July celebration. Call for more information.

- The park is handicapped accessible.

- Rest rooms and water fountains are located throughout the park.

Hours: Mid-April to early June and the last weekend in August: weekends only (Saturday, 10 a.m.-9 p.m.; Sunday, noon-9 p.m.). Mid-June to mid-August: daily except Monday (Tuesday-Saturday, 10 a.m.-9 p.m.; Sunday, noon-9 p.m.).

Admission: Gate admission for senior citizens (55 and older), $2. Regular admission, $6. A thrill ride ticket is $6 (in addition to general admission). Twilight admission (after 4 p.m.) is $3. Children ages 3 and younger are admitted free. For special group rates for 20 or more call 274-1776.

Directions: Conveniently located in the center of Memphis at the Mid-South Fairgrounds bounded by Central on the north, Southern on the south, Hollywood on the east and East Parkway on the west.

LICHTERMAN NATURE CENTER

5992 Quince Road
Memphis, Tennessee 38119 • 767-7322

You'll have to pinch yourself to make sure you're not just dreaming of a quiet, idyllic retreat while at Lichterman. It is almost unfathomable that such a refuge exists right in the midst of urban Memphis.

Accredited by the American Association of Museums, Lichterman Nature Center is a wildlife sanctuary and environmental education facility. Its 60 acres (originally owned by grocery magnate Clarence Saunders) offer safe haven (including a 12-acre lake) for creatures of forest, field, pond, and marsh habitats. The preserve allows visitors to observe native plants and animals in their natural settings. Expect to see something new each time you walk around at Lichterman—maybe animal tracks beside a stream or a turtle sunning on a log or a chipmunk scampering up a tree or... Exactly w*hat* you'll see can't be projected, but it is guaranteed that you'll encounter some fascinating animals and phenomena of nature on each visit to Lichterman. A few items that you might want to bring from home to enhance your visit are field guides, binoculars, or cameras.

Other than the rambling grounds themselves, points of particular interest at Lichterman include the Interpretive Center, housed in a historic Adirondack-style 1927 building with displays explaining the wonders of nature; the Greenhouse, where native wildflowers are propagated; the Ecology Room; the Discovery Room, offering such delights as nature games and the observation bee hive where real honey is being made; and the Rehabilitation Center, where injured wild animals are nurtured back to good health.

Frequent public tours are made available at Lichterman Nature Center. They are invariably very informative and very enjoyable. Watch the newspaper for dates and times or call Lichterman for more information.

- Brochures available.

- Tours take place in the form of weekend and daily nature walks guided by nature center staff member s— usually at 11 a.m. and 2 p.m. on Saturday and 2 p.m. on weekdays and Sunday. The schedule may change seasonally.

- Sufficient parking is available on the grounds. Special events may create crowding. Overflow parking is available off Lynnfield.

- Casual, long pants recommended, but not essential. Comfortable walking shoes should be worn. Visitors are asked to remain on designated trails when walking through the outdoor facility.

- Extensive environmental education programming is offered at Lichterman. Offerings change seasonally, but usually include "First Saturday" (for pre-third-graders), "Meet with Mother Nature," holiday activities, an after-school "SNOOPS" program, and others.

- There is a gift shop.

- Although no food concessions are available at Lichterman, there is a beautiful picnic area with tables overlooking the lake. Grills, open fires, or cooking of any kind is prohibited.

- Recycling bins are located in the picnic area.

- All buildings are handicapped accessible. Two short trails are paved and suitable for wheelchairs with some help. Strollers are welcome, but some trails have steps or obstacles that would make them difficult for stroller maneuvering.

- Rest rooms with large counters that can be used for changing diapers are available. A water fountain is available.

Hours: Tuesday-Saturday, 9:30 a.m.-5 p.m.; Sunday, 1-5 p.m.
Closed Mondays and all major winter holidays.

Admission: Adults, $3; children, college students with ID, and senior
citizens, $2; children 3 and under, free. Group rates
available with advance reservations. Free admission is
one of the many benefits of membership in the Memphis
Museum System.

Directions: From Poplar Avenue, turn south on Perkins, then left on
Quince. Lichterman Nature Center is between Lynnfield
and Ridgeway (due south of St. Francis Hospital).

THE MAGEVNEY HOUSE

198 Adams Avenue
Memphis, Tennessee 38103 • 526-4464

Possibly the oldest home in the city of Memphis and the site of Memphis's
first Catholic mass, the Magevney House was built in the mid-1830s. It
was bought in 1837 by Eugene Magevney, one of Memphis's first school
teachers and a founder of the city's public school system in 1848. His
daughter Kate was born here and lived here until her death in 1925. Kate
diversified her father's real estate holdings into stocks and bonds, building up a wealth that enabled her to give generously to many charitable
institutions in Memphis. In 1941 the house was given to the city of
Memphis by Kate's adopted daughter, Blanche Karsch.

The frugality of the Magevney family is evident in a tour of this quaint,
modest neighbor of the mansions farther east on Adams. The delightful
docents (look for Marie Brown, a font of history) are happy to share
stories about the hardships of the times, the trials of the Magevney family,
the tax situation that limited such things as closet space, and other

fascinating bits of Memphis lore. The striking restoration of the home includes flower arrangements made of human hair and sea shells, an ornate silver service, a harpsichord, family portraits, chamber pots, and kitchen crockery.

The gardens in the backyard offer an excellent, informative spot to wait for the beginning of a tour or to explore after a tour. Of particular interest are the scuppernong grape vines, the source of an old Memphis wine.

- Excellent brochure available at the end of the house tour.

- Tours are guided and take place on a flexible schedule. Reservations are suggested for group tours.

- Parking is available at pay lots across the street, or metered street parking is available.

- No food, drink, or flash cameras are allowed.

- The Magevney House holds periodic workshops (at a nominal charge) throughout the year, including Herb Gardening, Irish Dish Gardens, Victorian Christmas Crafts, Tatting, Lavender Lace, and Papier Mache Easter Eggs. Call for a schedule.

- Christmas and St. Patrick's Day merit special festivities at the Magevney House, with the staff dressing in period clothing. Music and storytelling occur throughout December.

- The Magevney House is not easily accessed by the handicapped.

- Rest rooms are available.

Hours: Tuesday-Saturday, 10 a.m.-4.p.m. Closed Sundays, Mondays, and major winter holidays. (Open 1-4 p.m. on Sundays during December.)

Admission: FREE (tax-deductible donations accepted).

Directions: Located in the heart of downtown Memphis on Adams Avenue just east of Third Street (one block from the Shelby County Courthouse).

MALIBU GRAND PRIX

6237 Shelby Oaks Drive
Memphis, Tennessee 38134 • 388-5780 (recorded message)
or 377-0548

Families looking for quick-paced excitement need look no further than the Malibu Grand Prix raceway. Located in east Memphis, this facility consists of a half-mile racetrack where the mini virage (go-carts), virage (scaled-down grand prix racers), and grand virage (two-seat racers) competitions take place. There are a few age and height restrictions for drivers and passengers, so be sure to check the information carefully so that no one is disappointed. Cars are computer-timed during each race.

For those less prone to living on the edge, or those just looking for a break from the speedway, there is a snack bar and game room within the facility.

- Saturday Madness takes place on Saturday afternoon. For $5 you can get 40 tokens, a hot dog, and a soft drink or 20 tokens plus two laps on the track.

- Mini virage drivers must be at least 4'6" tall. Virage drivers must be licensed drivers at least 16 years of age (parental consent also required for drivers under 18). Grand virage passengers must be at least 3'8" tall.

- Rest rooms and water fountains available.

Hours: Monday-Thursday, 11 a.m.-11 p.m.; Friday, 11 a.m.-midnight; Saturday, 10 a.m.-midnight; and Sunday, 10 a.m.-11p.m.

Admission: Before purchasing racecar laps, all drivers must purchase a "Malibu Racing License" for $2.75. (There is no admission charge for spectators or passengers.) Fees for mini virage are $2.25 per lap; virage packages are sold at $13.50 for seven laps or $18.50 for 11 laps; grand virage costs $2.85 per lap or $12.50 for five laps. (Discounted times are Monday-Friday from 4-7 p.m. and Sunday before noon, when mini virage or virage laps may be purchased at $1.75 each or grand virage laps at $2 each.)

Directions: Take I-240 to Exit 12 (Bartlett and Sycamore View Road). Turn left at the end of the ramp. Go right on Shelby Oaks Drive. Malibu Grand Prix is 3/4-mile farther, on the right-hand side of the street, next to Wimbleton Sportsplex.

THE MALLORY-NEELY HOUSE

652 Adams Avenue
Memphis, Tennessee 38105 • 523-1484

A superb example of the Italian villa architectural style, this mansion (ca. 1852) exemplifies the wealth accumulated by the city's leading families in the 19th century through local commodities. It is a showcase of High Victorian decorative arts, with the distinguishing feature that most of the furnishings and decoration of this house have survived intact a century or more because Frances Neely Mallory, the daughter of an early owner, resided here continuously until her death in 1969. Well-preserved are such beauties as the two elaborate stained-glass windows purchased by James Neely at the 1893 Chicago World's Fair. Also noteworthy in this former residence that is listed on the National Register of Historic Places

are the parquet floors, gilding, gaslights, stenciling, and carved mahogany fireplace mantels.

Visitors tour 10 rooms on the first and second floors of the three-story mansion plus the home's gardens, getting a glimpse of the actual surroundings of a wealthy Victorian family living a century ago. Children can get an idea of what day-to-day life was like for the Neely and Mallory families.

As a facility of the Memphis Park Commission and Memphis Museums, Inc., the Mallory-Neely House offers several special educational programs to groups and individuals through registration and fee payment. Among these are the Saturday Scholars Program (spring and fall semesters through Memphis State University), Halloween and Christmas events, and special exhibits at Christmas and during the summer.

- Excellent brochures are available at the gift shop (small building in the rear), where house tour tickets are purchased.

- Tours are guided and begin every 30 minutes from opening time till 3:30 p.m.

- Parking is at metered spaces on the street.

- Basic museum conservation rules apply: no touching, food, drink, flash photography.

- The Mallory-Neely House is available for private party rental.

- Picnicking on the grounds is allowed. No food concessions are available.

- Although the house is not highly accessible to the handicapped, the staff tries hard to provide accessibility. An advance call will reserve a parking space in the small staff lot, as well as first-floor special assistance. (No access to the second floor.)

- Rest rooms available.

Hours: Tuesday-Saturday, 10 a.m.-4 p.m.; Sunday, 1-4 p.m. (Closed Mondays and major winter holidays.)

Admission: Adults, $4; children, college students with ID, and senior citizens, $3; children under 5, free. (Reduced rates available for groups of 10 or more with advance reservations. Free admission for members of the Memphis Museum System; call 454-5607.)

Directions: Located between downtown Memphis and the medical center — two blocks south of Poplar — two blocks north of Madison.

MAYWOOD BEACH

8100 Maywood Drive
Olive Branch, Mississippi 38654 • 601-895-2777

If you thought the possibility of a white-sand beach in the middle of the United States, far removed from either coastline, was out of the question, then we have a surprise for you. Maywood Beach is just about 10 minutes from Memphis in Olive Branch, Mississippi. Opened in 1931, this popular "beach spot" is actually a huge swimming pool surrounded by acres of sand. Ten to fifteen acres of wooded property is adjacent to the beach, with picnic areas, concession stands, and shelter houses. This unusual beach locale provides not only the sun and fun of a sandy beach, but also the shady, cool benefits of a green forest.

Specializing in company picnics and school gatherings, Maywood offers group rates. Lifeguards are on duty at all times, and safety is emphasized.

•   Free parking is available.

- Shelters, picnic areas, and concession stands are available.

- You are allowed to bring your own picnic and other food supplies. But remember that glass is prohibited on beaches.

- Rest rooms and water fountains available.

Hours: Mid-May-Labor Day: daily (in late August — weekends only), Monday-Friday, 10 a.m.-6 p.m.; Saturday-Sunday, 10 a.m.-7 p.m.

Admission: Adults, $6.75; children 3-9, $4.75; children under 2, free.

Directions: Follow Highway 78 east from Memphis. Take the first exit after you enter Mississippi (Craft Road). Turn left and follow the signs to Maywood Beach.

MEEMAN-SHELBY STATE PARK

Millington, Tennessee 38053 • 876-5215

Popularly known to Memphians as Shelby Forest, this beautifully wooded park seeks to honor the memory of Edward J. Meeman, a one-time Memphis newspaper editor. The avid conservationist was instrumental in establishing this site as well as the Great Smoky Mountain National Park in eastern Tennessee.

With more than 20 miles of hiking and horseback trails and year-round fishing at the 125-acre Poplar Tree Lake, outdoor fun is around every turn!

The park boasts an Olympic-sized swimming pool, complemented by a wading pool for children. The pool is open from early summer through Labor Day, with lifeguards on duty during summer hours. The facility is served by a bathhouse and a concession stand.

Of course the campgrounds are an important feature of the park, and Meeman-Shelby State Park has not only 50 sites equipped with table, grill, and hook-up, but also six two-bedroom, fully equipped cabins located along the shore of Poplar Tree Lake. Although campsites are rented on a first-come, first-served basis, they can be reserved well in advance; cabins, too, should be reserved in advance at the visitor center.

Some of the numerous recreational activities enjoyed at Meeman-Shelby State Park are field games, volleyball, badminton, horseshoes, disc golf, and softball. Recreation equipment and games may be checked out free of charge at the visitor center or the nature center.

• Brochures and maps are available.

• Rental jonboats are available at boat docks. Personally owned boats with electric motors are allowed on the lake for a small launch fee, but no gasoline motors are allowed. A free boat launch is also available on the Mississippi River.

• A park fishing permit is required, in addition to a valid Tennessee fishing license, for anyone over 16 years of age.

• Park naturalists provide many programs such as special arts and crafts displays, guided tours, pioneer living demonstrations, or-

ganized games, movies, hayrides, and square dancing. Check with the park office for schedules.

- 300 picnic tables and grills are located throughout the park. Picnic shelters and group camps can be rented for large gatherings.

- A nature center containing natural history exhibits and displays is open from early summer through Labor Day and at other times by appointment.

- Handicapped accessible.

- Rest rooms and water fountains available.

Hours: Summer, 8 a.m.-10 p.m. (Tuesday 10 a.m.-6:30 p.m.); winter, 8 a.m.-sundown. (Camper quiet time begins at 10 p.m.)

Admission: Free admission to the beautiful park itself. Nominal fees for special recreational activities listed above.

Directions: Located within Shelby County, 15 miles north of Memphis, near Millington — off U.S. Highway 51 (North Watkins) on Bluff Road.

MEMPHIS BOTANIC GARDEN

750 Cherry Road
Memphis, Tennessee 38117 • 685-1566

Memphis Botanic Garden got its start in 1953 with the iris garden. In 1964 the Goldsmith Foundation dedicated the building on the property, Goldsmith Civic Center, to the memory of Jacob Goldsmith, founder of Goldsmith's Department Stores. The Civic Center serves as a meeting facility for Mid-South plant societies and garden clubs and as the office headquarters for the Botanic Garden. With 20 display gardens, an arboretum, an orchid greenhouse, an organic garden, azalea and dogwood trails, and much more, this "tranquil preserve" acts as an educational institution through displays and special programs and plays a leading role in the city's environmental awareness.

"Grand Openings Everyday!" Memphis Botanic Garden's slogan holds true in all seasons. Suggested viewing times for the major gardens are: May till the first frost for the Rose Garden; the end of April through the first of May for the Iris Garden (one of the largest in the United States); April for the Wildflower Woodlands; spring, summer, and fall for the Perennial and Herb Gardens; June for the Cactus and Day Lily Gardens; and any time of year for the Japanese and Sensory Gardens.

Feeding the Koi fish in the Japanese Garden is a particular delight for children. (Fish food may be purchased at the vending feeders at the bridge.) Photographing the plants and fish is another popular family activity here. Trams, which operate on a fluctuating schedule, provide a restful guided tour of the lovely gardens at a modest fee.

The major annual events at Memphis Botanic Garden are the Spring Plant Sale (April), the Good Earth Festival (June), the Fall Plant Sale (October), and the Holiday Decoration Show (December).

A visit to the Botanic Garden at any time of year provides a wholesome, educational experience for the entire family. The facility fosters an appreciation for the natural environment. The ambitious master plan will add even more delights and new features in the near future.

- Brochures available in the Civic Center.

- Tram tours are available on a flexible schedule.

- There is plenty of free parking in the lot, with room for buses and vans.

- Picnic tables on the grounds offer an excellent *al fresco* dining spot. The lakeside pavilion is available, through paid reservations, for such gatherings as family reunions.

- The property is fully accessible to the handicapped.

- Rest rooms and water fountain available.

Hours: Tuesday-Saturday, 9 a.m.-sunset; Sunday, 11 a.m.-6 p.m. (Closed Mondays and major winter holidays.)

Admission: Adults, $2; senior citizens (65+), $1.50; children 6-17 or full-time students with ID, $1; children under 6, free. Group rates available (minimum 15). MBG Foundation members free. (Admission fees waived on Tuesdays from 12:30 till sunset.)

Directions: Located in Audubon Park, which is one block south of Poplar at Perkins. Approach Cherry Road from Park Avenue or Southern Avenue.

MEMPHIS BROOKS MUSEUM OF ART

Overton Park
Memphis, Tennessee 38112 • 722-3500

As Tennessee's oldest and largest museum of fine arts, Memphis Brooks Museum of Art, houses a permanent collection that spans antiquity to the present and includes painting, sculpture, prints, photographs, drawings, and decorative arts. The award-winning building features a large rotunda entry area, exposed marble walls with carved figures, and a dining terrace overlooking Overton Park. Innovative programming ensures that even the youngest visitors to the museum will explore and discover.

In addition to the museum's permanent collection, major exhibitions of both widely recognized artists and just-emerging talents change every six to eight weeks. A recent exhibition of the drawings and watercolors of Jean and Laurent deBrunhoff, called The Art of Babar, fascinated children familiar with the lovable, royal elephant. Many participated in the full range of programs and family events that were planned to complement the exhibition.

Among the museum's other special features are the galleries **In Touch with Art**, where visitors can feel actual works of art, and **Your Point of View: Another Way to See Art,** which provides family activity sheets and hands-on creative opportunities to go along with the changing exhibits.

*   Brochures about Brooks, current exhibits, and upcoming events are available.

*   Docent-led tours are available each Saturday at 1:30 p.m. and each Sunday at 1:30 and 4 p.m. Group tours may be scheduled by calling 722-3515. Tours for hearing-impaired or visually impaired visitors are available by appointment.

*   Free parking is available in a paved lot to the northeast of the building and on surrounding streets.

*   Shirt and shoes are required. Children under 12 should be accompanied by an adult.

*   There is an outstanding museum gift shop facing the large rotunda entrance that features art-related gift items including jewelry, illustrated art books, handmade toys, posters, and local pottery.

*   Weekend family workshops are offered, as well as annual holiday performance series featuring music, dance, theatre, and film.

*   The Brushmark Restaurant, located just off the rotunda entrance, serves affordably priced luncheons Tuesday-Sunday from 11:30 a.m. to 3:30 p.m. For reservations call 276-6759.

- The museum is fully accessible to the handicapped with exterior ramps and elevators to all floors.

- Rest rooms and water fountains available.

Hours: Tuesday-Saturday, 10 a.m.-5 p.m.; Sunday, 11:30 a.m.-5 p.m. Closed Mondays and major winter holidays.

Admission: Adults, $4; students 6-25 with ID, $2; senior citizens (over 55), $2; children under 5, free. Group rates are available. Admission waived on Fridays. (Memphis Brooks Museum membership offers many privileges, one being free admission to the museum. Ask for details about various levels of membership at admission desk.)

Directions: Centrally located in Overton Park, off Poplar Avenue, just west of East Parkway and five miles from downtown Memphis.

MEMPHIS MUSIC AND BLUES MUSEUM

97 S. Second Street
Memphis, Tennessee 38103 • 525-4007

This unassuming little museum sets down in a no-frills repository an unbelievable collection of memorabilia from the Memphis area's musical past. Opened in the summer of 1991, the museum occupies the former home of an antique shop across the street from The Peabody Hotel.

Listing the highlights of the collection is next-to-impossible because there are simply so many rare and unusual items from the local music industry. Display cases are somewhat eclectic, with blues greats sharing space with rock 'n' roll favorites. There are numerous video and audio tapes that run continuously and can be heard through individual earphones attached to the display cases in which they are located.

Features of special interest include rare photographs and recordings; victrolas; musical instruments from clarinets and trumpets to guitars, washboards, and harmonicas; several jukeboxes; Roaring '20s costumes; a cotton-picking sack and scales; liquor jugs; a vaudeville display; a gospel music exhibit; a shoe-shine stand; . . . As we said, there are far too many to list. Names to look for include B.B. King, Furry Lewis, James "Son" Thomas, "Little" Laura Dukes, T-Bone Walker, Johnny Cash, Bo Diddley (ask for the story about his guitar on display), and Roy Orbison.

Don't come here looking for fancy displays and slick promotions. But if your family is fascinated by the blues music that originated in Memphis and the other diverse elements of our music industry, this museum will leave you spellbound.

- Brochures at the front desk.

- Tours are available by reservation. Otherwise, visitors self-guide and are at liberty to ramble at will.

- This is a Downtown attraction, with parking available only at metered street spots or in nearby pay lots.

- There is a small, touristy gift shop at the entrance, as well as a well-stocked guitar shop featuring vintage equipment for sale.

- Handicapped accessible.

- Rest rooms and water fountain available.

Hours: January-March: Sunday-Thursday, 11 a.m.-5 p.m.; Friday-Saturday, 11 a.m.-9 p.m. April-December: Sunday-Thursday, 11 a.m.-6 p.m.; Friday-Saturday, 11 a.m.-9 p.m.

Admission: $5; children under 12, free.

Directions: Across the street from The Peabody Hotel on Second
Street (1 1/2 blocks from Beale Street).

MEMPHIS PINK PALACE MUSEUM AND PLANETARIUM

3050 Central Avenue
Memphis, Tennessee 38111 • 320-6320

The Memphis Pink Palace Museum gets its name from the pink
marble mansion that grocery entrepreneur Clarence Saunders (founder
of Piggly Wiggly) built as a private residence in the 1920s. The mansion,
never actually resided in by the family, went to the city when the Saunders'
fortunes failed, and it housed the permanent exhibits and museum
collections until they were moved in 1977 to the 67,000-square-foot
contemporary facility built on the grounds at that time. The Pink Palace
Planetarium is located in the more recent facility, while the mansion now
contains one of the best-equipped museum education departments in the
country. Currently expanding once more (at a cost of over $14 million),
the new Changing Exhibits Hall is under construction and will open in
May 1992 with an exhibit of art and archaeology from the Vatican
peninsula.

Among the largest museums in the Southeast, the Pink Palace focuses on
the cultural and natural history of the Mid-South. Exhibits detail what life
was like in Memphis in the 1840s, which mammals flourished here and
which died out, what life in the "small world" under a microscope is like,
and more.

An exact replica of Clarence Saunders' 1916 Piggly Wiggly allows a make-
believe visit to the world's first self-service grocery store. Clyde Parke's
fascinating, animated toy circus brings to life hundreds of handmade
pieces under the big top.

Other highlights of the museum include "Memphis: 1800-1900," "From

Saddlebags to Science: A Century of Health Care in Memphis," and "Geology: 4.6 Billion Years of Earth History." The Changing Exhibit Hall offers a feast of rotating new subjects for exciting exploration.

The Memphis Pink Palace Planetarium presents a variety of entertaining, informative programs on astronomy. The dramatic theatre-in-the-round zooms visitors to foreign lands and through wide galaxies. Space science becomes a reality through the star projector, abetted by the viewers' imagination. Shows change frequently, so expect a new adventure with each visit.

- Brochures are available.

- Spacious lot provides ample free parking.

- Fantastic summer day camps and mini sessions, as well as school-year Saturday programs, for children of all ages. Call 320-6363 for more information.

- No barefoot visitors allowed.

- New gift shop and snack bar under construction, opening in 1992.

- Fully accessible to the handicapped.

- Rest rooms and water fountains available.

Hours: Museum: Tuesday-Friday, 9:30 a.m.-4:30 p.m.; Thursday, 9:30 a.m.-8:30 p.m.; Saturday, 9:30 a.m.-5:00 p.m.; Sunday, 1:00-5:00 p.m. Closed Mondays and major winter holidays. Planetarium shows: Saturday, 11 a.m., 1:30 p.m., 2:45 p.m.; Sunday, 1:30 p.m., 2:45 p.m., 4 p.m.

Admission: Adults, $3; children, college students, and senior citizens, $2; children 4 and under, free. Planetarium admission is $2.50 and $1.75. Package rates for museum and planetarium are $4.50 and $3.25. Group rates are available with advance reservations. Prices are subject to change.

(Memphis Museum System membership offers many benefits, including free admission to the Pink Palace, the Mallory-Neely House, and Lichterman Nature Center.)

Directions: In midtown Memphis on Central Avenue at Lafayette.

MEMPHIS POLICE MUSEUM

159 Beale Street
Memphis, Tennessee 38103 • 528-2370

The Police Museum, located in a 150-year-old building that was once a men's clothing store, is the only such museum in the nation that houses an active police sub-station which provides 24-hour police service.

More than one hundred years' worth of law enforcement history is presented in the museum. Police equipment, confiscated weapons, photographs of notorious lawbreakers, criminal records, mug shots, a fingerprint machine, and other interesting items surround the authentic jail cell featured in the museum. A close examination of ominous-looking drug paraphernalia here should encourage youngsters to say an emphatic NO. The officer on duty will be happy to pass along to children a free copy the anti-drug coloring book distributed by the Crime Prevention Bureau of the Memphis Police Department.

- An informative flyer is available on request at the duty sergeant's desk.

- Tours, including drug lectures, are available by reservation.

- Look for free parking in the lots behind the shops and restaurants on the south side of Beale.

- Although pets, food, and drink are prohibited in the museum, cameras are welcome. (Photo opportunity at the jail cell.)

- Sidewalk-level access for the handicapped, but narrow entrance to the museum.

- No public rest rooms, but water fountain is available.

Hours: Daily, 24 hours a day.

Admission: FREE.

Directions: Between Second and Third Streets on Beale in downtown Memphis.

MEMPHIS QUEEN LINE

Foot of Monroe Avenue at Riverside Drive
P.O. Box 3188
Memphis, Tennessee 38177-0188 • 527-5694

What better way to see and experience the mighty Mississippi River than a sightseeing cruise on one of the five paddlewheel boats owned by the Memphis Queen Line!

A live commentary of the history, sights, and legends of the Mississippi is given by the Captain on this 1 1/2-hour cruise. Points of interest along the way include President's Island, the Frisco Railroad Bridge, Waterways Marine, The Pyramid, the Church on the River, and much more.

The Memphis Queen Line also offers a Sunset Dinner Cruise featuring Big Band and Dixieland music at 7 p.m. Wednesday-Sunday, May-September. Call ahead for more information.

Other cruises, such as the Moonlight Dance Cruise starting at 10:30 p.m. Friday and Saturday nights (May through September), are offered, although not child-oriented. Call for more information.

• Brochures available.

• Parking on the cobblestone lot is part of the treat of a visit to the river. Some skill required, but parking is free and interesting.

• Concessions and gift counters available on all boats.

• Memphis Queen Line boats can be rented for private parties and other special events, such as reunions, weddings, etc.

• There is no refund of tickets or fares unless a cruise is completely cancelled as a result of unforeseen circumstances.

• Handicapped accessible.

• Rest rooms available, water available on request.

Hours: The 1 1/2-hour sightseeing cruise schedule varies from month to month. With the exception of the last week of December and all of January and February, when the boats are not in operation, there is a 2:30 p.m. cruise every day of the week. There are also 4:30 p.m. weekend cruises in late spring and early fall months. The summer months offer these schedules, as well as a weekday morning cruise (10:30 a.m.) and an early evening cruise (6:30 p.m.) every day. Schedules are subject to change. Exact schedules are available in brochures or by telephone.

Admission: Costs for the 1 1/2-hour sightseeing cruise are: adults and children 12 and over, $7.50; senior citizens 55 and over, $7; children 4-11, $4.50; children under 3 with parents, free. Prices are subject to change.

Directions: Located on the Mississippi River at the foot of Monroe Avenue in downtown Memphis.

THE MEMPHIS ZOO AND AQUARIUM

Overton Park
Memphis, Tennessee 38112 • 726-4775

The Memphis Zoo, a wonderful place for families, is Memphis's most popular public attraction, drawing more than 500,000 visitors a year. The zoo knows no limitations of age, gender, education, race, or income. Everyone loves the zoo!

Founded in 1906 to house a southern black bear named Natchez, the Memphis Zoo is currently undergoing a major renovation that will double its size and make it one of the country's best. It is now recognized internationally for its role in preserving many endangered species. With more than 2,800 animals representing 400 species, the zoo will add the free-roaming Cat Country in the spring of 1993. An already-completed renovation is the impressive 40-foot tall, 162-foot wide Egyptian-style entrance (playing up, of course, the connection between Memphis on the Nile and Memphis on the Mississippi) and the giant animal cracker-style Avenue of Animals leading to the entrance.

A delightful attraction at the zoo that has been popular literally for generations (today's adults once enjoyed it as much as their children are doing a few decades later) is the children's ride area with pint-sized boats, trains, and swinging baskets, to name a few. Another favorite with families is the children's zoo, where some petting is allowed. Llamas, cattle, kangaroos, and others provide close-up entertainment.

Educational activities at the zoo include animal feeding times (designated daily), sea lion and birds of prey shows, docents' "touch carts," and self-guided exploration (docents stationed strategically to answer visitors' questions). Summer Zoo Camp and puppet shows are seasonal treats. Special fund-raising events, some of which cater primarily to adults, include Zoo Grass (June music festival), Zoo Rendezvous (major fund-raising gala), Zoo Boo (Halloween party), Winter Lights (December illumination), and the annual Members' Night Party (behind-the-scenes nighttime tour).

- Brochures available at gate.

- Guided tours available for groups with reservations. Call 725-4768.

- Ample parking is available on spacious lots at the entrance. There is a weekend parking fee of $1, which is refunded with zoo admission.

- No glass bottles or straws are allowed in the zoo.

- The gift shop features a variety of animal-related items.

- Snack bars offering hamburgers, hot dogs, chicken, and such fare, as well as numerous picnic tables, are available at the zoo.

- The zoo is handicapped accessible. Strollers and wheelchairs may be rented.

• Rest rooms and water fountains available.

Hours: April-September: daily, 9 a.m.-5 p.m. October-March: daily, 9 a.m.-4:30 p.m.

Admission: Zoo: adults, $4; children 2-11 and senior citizens, $2; children under 2, free. Admission is waived on Mondays after 3:30. Aquarium: ages 6-11, 10 cents; ages 12 and up, 25 cents. Free admission to the zoo is one of the many benefits included in membership packages. Call 276-9453 for membership information.

Directions: From Poplar Avenue (just east of McLean Boulevard), enter Overton Park at the light at Kenilworth. Follow the signs to the parking lot, which is straight ahead. Or from McLean, turn east on Galloway, and drive directly to the parking lot.

MISSISSIPPI RIVER ADVENTURE

The western boundary for the state of Tennessee
And the city of Memphis

Believing "Old Man River" deserves an entry all its own in this second chapter, we have set out to give you an overall view of Memphis's premiere natural attraction.

First let's look at the river's history and geographic significance. The Mississippi, which is the longest river in the United States, is also the chief river of North America. Spanish explorer Hernando de Soto was the first European to travel the river, when he crossed near Memphis in 1541. The bridge at the north end of the city has been named after this famous explorer.

The Mississippi River was named by the Native Americans, including the Illinois, the Kickapoo, and the Ojibway, who lived in the upper Mississippi valley. Their "big river" (the meaning of Mississippi) can be traveled by boats for over 1800 miles — from Minneapolis, Minnesota, to the Gulf of Mexico. Native American tribes of the lower Mississippi Valley included the Chickasaw, the Choctaw, the Natchez, and the Tunica.

Ranging in depth from nine feet to 100 feet, the river is always bustling with activity. Most commercial freight — consisting of coal and steel going south; corn, soybeans, and wheat headed north — travels on large barges pushed by tugboats. Muskrats and opossums are everyday sights along the river banks. The Mississippi River drains an area of 1.25 million square miles in 31 states. The U.S. Corps of Engineers is charged with the responsibility for maintaining the navigability and flood control along the Mississippi River.

In 1871, when the river's importance to the burgeoning transportation and trade industries was growing with the development of steamboats, Congress decided to determine a set point for the lowest river level. This constant point around which other water levels in the Mississippi are measured is called 0 gauge reading. (At the time of the setting, 0 was the lowest reference level on record. But since then, the river has occasionally dropped several feet below this "lowest" level.) At 30 feet above this river stage, the water starts leaving its channel. By 34 feet above 0, the river is at flood stage.

Now when the water recedes to 10 feet above 0 or all the way down to 3 or 4 feet below 0, the river is said to be low. At this time, you can explore the banks of the Mississippi and see the debris and marks left behind by the previously swollen, flowing body of water. (You can determine the river stage by looking at the gauge reading that is posted on the bluff directly across Riverside Drive from Tom Lee Park or by checking the weather report in the daily newspaper.) The next time the river gets down to low levels, try this adventure.

Take the very first left after crossing the old Memphis-Arkansas Bridge. Follow the road south underneath the bridge pilings until the road ends. You have found **Engineers' Park.** This is a large sandbar on the Arkansas side of the river, across from Presidents Island. During your exploration you should be able to see interesting variations left by the shifting stream, with high points and gravel bars. Looking upstream, you can see a Corps of Engineers rock dike and bank revetments used for river stability.

There are many magnificent views from almost every point on both sides of the Mississippi. Parks overlooking the river dot the Memphis bluffs. **Ashburn Park,** high on the South Bluff, gives an expansive view of the river. Try finding your own favorite spot to view a scenic panorama. Remember to practice river safety even on the banks, which are sometimes unstable at the water's edge, and on the sandbars. Wading or swimming in the Mississippi River is hazardous in spite of the deceptively calm appearance of the water. Shifting sands and swift, powerful currents have even undermined dry sandbars.

MUD ISLAND

125 N. Front Street
Memphis, Tennessee 38103 • 576-7241

Across Wolf River from its Front Street entrance, Mud Island (actually a peninsula rather than an island, but who cares about such technicalities?) offers visitors the choice of a ride on its futuristic monorail or a walk over the river on the screened-in pedestrian bridge. Either mode of transportation provides a fascinating bird's-eye view of the waters below.

Once on Mud Island, guests may choose from an assortment of delightful attractions, one being the unique **Mississippi River Walk,** a five-block-long scale model of the mighty river. Another treasure is the 18-gallery **Mississippi River Museum,** featuring 10,000 years of river life, legends, and folklore vividly displayed as part of the River Center. On the north end of the facility the **Memphis Belle Pavilion** provides a comfortable resting place for World War II's most famous B-17 bomber.

Other features of Mud Island include the 5,000-seat amphitheater, gift shops, restaurants, and the Bud Boogie Beach swimming pool/beach area.

- Call for tour and group rate information.

- Mud Island's pay parking lot is located at the Front Street entrance. Limited metered street parking is also available.

- Shirts and shoes are required, except on playing field. No cutoffs allowed in swimming pool.

- Although cameras may be taken into the museum, no flash photography is permitted.

- All areas are accessible to guests in wheelchairs.

- Rest rooms and water fountains are available.

Hours: Mud Island is closed during the winter months, and the hours of operation for the business season vary from year to year. Visitors are requested to call 576-7241 for current information.

Admission: Varies from year to year. Call 576-7241 for current information.

Directions: Mud Island is located on the western border of downtown Memphis. From Poplar Avenue, drive due west until the street ends at the entrance to Mud Island's parking lot.

NATIONAL CIVIL RIGHTS MUSEUM

450 Mulberry Street
Memphis, Tennessee 38103 (Site of the Lorraine Motel) • 521-9699

One of the newest museums in Memphis is the National Civil Rights Museum, which is housed in the former Lorraine Motel, the site of the assassination of Dr. Martin Luther King. Committed to non-violence, Dr. King was the foremost leader of our nation's struggle in the 1960s with civil rights. People come from around the world to pay tribute to Dr. King and the far-reaching movement he led.

Following Dr. King's death in 1968, the motel fell into disrepair and continued to deteriorate. Finally, in 1982 a small group of black community members, including Circuit Judge D'Army Bailey, joined together to preserve the site and begin the formation of the National Civil Rights Museum. Now owned by the State of Tennessee, the museum offers the first comprehensive overview of the American civil rights movement in exhibit form.

"Movement to Overcome," a bronze sculpture by Michael Pavlovsky, is located in the lobby of the museum. Civil rights exhibits of the 1950s and 1960s include the March on Washington, Freedom Rides, the Montgomery Bus Boycott (featuring a full-size bus reproduction), Student Sit-ins, the Battle for Ole Miss, and the Reverend Dr. Martin Luther King. The museum brings to life some of the most significant aspects of modern American history. Visitors witness the sights, sounds, and tensions of the civil rights movement.

The National Civil Rights Museum gives children the opportunity to view exhibits and see films on events that, before now, they have only heard about from older family members and friends.

- Brochure available.

- Group tours can be arranged through advance reservations.

- Suggested preparatory reading: *Eyes on the Prize: America's Civil Rights Years 1954-1965* by Juan Williams.

- Parking is available at the lot on Mulberry Street.

- Gift shop near the lobby.

- Ongoing educational programming includes lectures, exhibits, speakers, and special performances. A calendar of events is published quarterly.

- Handicapped accessible.

- Rest rooms and water fountains available.

Hours: Monday-Saturday, 10 a.m.-5 p.m.; Sunday, 1-5 p.m. (Sunday hours extended to 6 p.m. June-August.) Closed Tuesdays.

Admission: Adults, $5; senior citizens and students with ID, $4; children 6-12, $3. FREE on Mondays 3-5 p.m. Group rates available.

Directions: Coming south on Second Street, turn right on Vance, then left on Mulberry Street.

NATIONAL ORNAMENTAL METAL MUSEUM

374 West California
Memphis, Tennessee 38106 • 774-6380

The National Ornamental Metal Museum is the only institution of its kind in the United States dedicated to collecting, exhibiting, and preserving fine metalwork of all kinds. An exciting series of changing exhibits, featuring all forms of metal from jewelry and hollowware to Renaissance armor and architectural wrought iron, is offered. Educational programs range from classes to daily metalworking demonstrations in the Schering-Plough smithy located on the grounds.

Unlike most museums, this one offers visitors the opportunity to see how objects in the galleries were made and to talk with working crafts makers. The flash and fire of the process is particularly appealing to children.

The museum's entry gates involved more than 150 metalsmiths from 14 nations. They were designed by Richard Quinnell of Surrey, England, and commemorate the museum's tenth anniversary in 1989. The grounds afford a spectacular view of the Mississippi River, described by Mark Twain as "the finest between Cairo and New Orleans." Picnic tables, cast-iron garden furniture, and outdoor sculpture set down among large shade trees make this an ideal location for visitors who bring a picnic lunch with them.

• Brochures are available.

• Tours are self-paced. Guided tours, followed by demonstrations by staff artists, are available to groups with advance reservations.

• Ample free parking is available on the street.

- Standard museum etiquette applies in the gallery building; dress code is casual.

- Popular regular events include "Repair Days" (third weekend in October) and the blacksmithing classes and special metal work shops scheduled in the fall and spring. Special exhibits change every seven to nine weeks.

- There is a gift shop with a variety of items, including unusual metal artwork.

- Soda vending machines in the smithy; no other food services available.

- Handicap access to the gift shop, first-floor galleries, rest rooms, smithy, and grounds; no elevator to second-floor gallery.

- Rest rooms and water fountain available.

Hours: Tuesday-Saturday, 10 a.m.-5 p.m.; Sunday, noon-5 p.m. (except when closed for exhibit changes — call ahead).

Admission: Adults, $2; senior citizens (62+), $1; children (5-18), 75 cents; children under 5, free. Members entitled to free admission. Admission fees waived on Wednesdays from 10 a.m. till noon. (Tax-deductible donations welcomed.)

Directions: Just south of downtown Memphis — Crump Boulevard west toward the Memphis-Arkansas (I-55) bridge; right on Delaware (Exit 12-C); two blocks south on Delaware to West California; turn right. Museum is one block down on California on the riverbluff.

THE ORPHEUM

203 South Main
Memphis, Tennessee 38103 • 525-7800 or 525-3000

This magnificent theatre was built in 1927-28 at a cost of $1,600,000 to replace the Grand Opera House, which had been built on this lot in 1907 and burned down in 1923. A member of the Orpheum Circuit of Vaudeville Theatres, it was the site of performances by all the big-name vaudeville stars of the '20s. In 1940 the theatre was closed as a result of the decline in popularity of vaudeville, then purchased by the Malco chain as a movie theatre. In 1976 the non-profit Memphis Development Foundation acquired use of the then-abandoned building from the city and raised $5,000,000 in 1982 for its restoration. The opulently refurbished "opera house" was re-opened in 1984 and, since then, has hosted more Broadway touring shows than any other theatre in the country.

The Orpheum boasts of being Memphis's first civic landmark. It was designed by the Chicago architectural firm of Rapp and Rapp, who specialized in French design. This Italian building is, then, the exception to their usual design.

Some of the outstanding features to look for in the Orpheum include the extensive gold leafing (seven layers, all told); the "mighty" Wurlitzer organ installed in 1928 to accompany the silent movies; the 15-foot tall, 2,000-pound chandeliers of hand-cut Czechoslovakian crystal (purchased in 1927 at a cost of $37,000 each); and the meticulously restored carpet with every thread as close to the original design as possible.

Those who are superstitious might also be on the lookout for "Mary," the resident ghost, who is said by those who stand behind their sightings that she is an adolescent with long brown braids, a white dress, and black stockings. She is reported to be friendly. The Orpheum family (Friends of the Orpheum) is also reported to be among the friendliest groups

71

visited by the Broadway touring companies, who look forward during their stay in Memphis to home-cooked meals for the entire cast and crew.

- Tours of the Orpheum can be arranged for groups of 20 or more. Fees vary, but average $1 per person. Arrangements must be made by advance call, and tours are always subject to availability.

- Limited on-street free parking is available after 5 p.m. Nearby lots provide adequate parking for a fee.

- Even though refreshments are offered in the lobby during performance intermissions, no food or drink is allowed inside the theatre.

- There is no permanent gift shop, but the Friends of the Orpheum provide a gift booth at most performances.

- Some of the special events at the Orpheum are: two Broadway series each year (eight shows all together), the summer movie series, a fall fund-raising auction, Opera Memphis productions, Memphis Concert Ballet performances, varied school shows (such as "The Pied Piper").

- The Orpheum is handicapped accessible.

- There are rest rooms and water fountains.

Hours: Varies with performance (or by special arrangement for groups of 20 or more).

Admission: Varies with performance (generally $4-$5 per person for movies, upwards of $35 for national touring productions).

Directions: Located on the southwest corner of Main and Beale streets in downtown Memphis.

OVERTON PARK

Poplar at East Parkway
Memphis, Tennessee 38112

Overton Park sits squarely in the center of several historic neighborhoods of Memphis and for over 90 years has entertained generations of Memphians and residents of the surrounding three-state area. Major attractions located within the 342-acre park are Memphis Brooks Museum of Art (see listing in this chapter), Memphis Zoo and Aquarium (see listing in this chapter), and Memphis College of Art (see listing in Chapter 3).

Beautiful winding nature trails, jogging paths, and bike trails, in addition to picnic facilities, are marked throughout the park. Open spaces sit waiting for a Frisbee tournament, an afternoon of kite-flying, or a simple game of catch. Soccer and baseball fields can be reserved through the park commission (day use permits at 325-7615, night use permits at 325-7616). Rainbow Lake, a small constructed body of water designed for scenic beauty, has playground equipment nearby. (Swimming or wading in Rainbow Lake would be unsafe and is prohibited.) Another playground is located on the east side of the park near the large gazebo. Rest rooms are available at both areas.

Of historical interest within the park is the World War I Dough Boy statue, erected by the Memphis Daughters of the American Revolution on a site near the playing fields. Also of interest is the statue near Brooks Museum of Edward Hull Crump, long-time mayor of Memphis and leader of a major political machine of the early decades of the 20th century.

A public golf course borders the south side of the park and is the site of one of the more popular junior tournaments in Memphis.

The Raoul Wallenberg Shell, situated between Brooks Museum and Memphis College of Art, is an outdoor amphitheater that comes to life with such diverse entertainment as jazz concerts, ballet performances, and chamber music.

- Parking is available throughout the park. A special lot is designated for zoo parking.

- Arts in the Park, a festival that takes place in mid-October, is one of a variety of special events that occur in the park.

- Rest rooms and water fountains are available near shelters and playgrounds.

Hours: Open 6 a.m.-midnight.

Admission: FREE.

Directions: Located in midtown Memphis, Overton Park is bordered by Poplar Avenue on the south, McLean on the west, North Parkway on the north, and East Parkway on the east.

THE PEABODY

149 Union Avenue
Memphis, Tennessee 38103 • 529-4000

The Peabody is one of the grand hotels of the South, full of southern tradition and history. From the famous ducks in the lobby to the dancing on the roof, The Peabody is a living, breathing, stylish legend.

Listed on the National Register of Historic Places, this Italian Renaissance

Revival structure was opened in 1869, rebuilt in 1925, and recently restored to its legendary elegance. The five entrances open into a two-story lobby that is dominated by an opulent fountain carved from a single piece of travertine marble. This fountain is the home of The Peabody's longest continuous guests — The Peabody Ducks.

Left in the fountain originally as a joke, these web-footed celebrities have delighted both young and old. Marching down from their Penthouse Palace each morning to spend the day charming visitors at their fountain home, then marching back up each evening, The Peabody Ducks have held a position of honor in this 50-year-old tradition.

Four award-winning restaurants are located within The Peabody: Chez Philippe (classic French cuisine), Dux (American food and wine), Cafe Expresso (Viennese pastry shop/New York deli), and Mallards Bar and Grill (casual lunch or dinner). Weekend entertainment is also offered. The Skyway, an art deco-style ballroom, and the Plantation Roof offer breathtaking views of the city.

- Brochure available.

- Short-term metered street parking is available, as well as lot parking at The Peabody. Rates fluctuate. There is an additional fee for valet service.

- A wonderful gift shop is located in the lobby, along with several other specialty shops.

- Appropriate attire is expected. Guests may be casually dressed. Some of the restaurants require more formal attire.

- The hotel is host to many special events throughout the year. Some favorites include the summer Sunset Serenades on the roof, holiday Christmas caroling, Christmas tree lighting, Easter egg hunt, a Halloween bash, and New Year's Eve celebration.

- The hotel and all its restaurants are handicapped accessible. Handicapped accessible rooms are available.

- Rest rooms and water fountains are available.

Hours: The hotel is always open. The Peabody Ducks march at 11 a.m. and 5 p.m. (Get there early in order not to miss the Grand Entrance or Grand Exit. The ducks are prompt.)

Admission: FREE admission to the hotel and duck parade. Fees charged for some of the special events.

Directions: Located in the heart of Memphis's business district at the corner of Union and Second Avenues, five blocks from Cook Convention Center

THE PYRAMID

One Auction Avenue
Memphis, Tennessee 38103 • 521-9675

Opened in November, 1991, The Pyramid is destined to be a major distinguishing feature of Memphis, Tennessee, and a reminder of the Egyptian city whose name we proudly bear. This glistening landmark beckons travelers across the Hernando de Soto bridge from its majestic perch on the banks of the Mississippi River. Thirty-two stories tall, it could hold 200,000,000 gallons of water!

The featured attraction of The Pyramid is its arena. This sports and entertainment facility holds 22,500 upholstered, cushioned seats, where Memphis State University Tiger basketball fans, as well as spectators at touring family shows, concerts, and community events, can enjoy their view in comfort.

- Parking lot on north and south sides of The Pyramid.

- Variety of food offered at 10 permanent concession stands plus additional portable facilities.

- Full accessibility to the handicapped. (Enter from the south side.)

- Rest rooms and water fountains available.

Hours: Open for sports and other special events.

Admission: Varies with event.

Directions: West on Poplar Avenue to Front Street. Right on Front. The Pyramid is on the left at Auction.

A. SCHWAB

163 Beale Street
Memphis, Tennessee 38103 • 523-9782

We defy you to come up with an unusual item of days-gone-by that cannot be found at A. Schwab's dry goods store. The business, established in 1876 by Abraham Schwab, remains a family enterprise run by Abraham's grandson Abram and granddaughter Eleanor. The 1911 building has hardly changed in the past few decades, and many of the goods available for purchase are more than a little reminiscent of the '50s and earlier.

Where else can you expect to find backscratchers; deerstalker caps (for Sherlock Holmes buffs); denim overalls; "penny" candy; Memphis playing cards; packaged cotton bolls; an assortment of suspenders, straw hats, spools of thread, cards of buttons; and a wild array of diverse souvenirs, jewelry, clothing, food, and books? We cannot promise that you'll find everything (or even anything) you need at A. Schwab's, but we can guarantee that you'll find something to amuse and please.

The mezzanine level of the store features the "museum," where you'll find old records, farm implements, cooking equipment, antique clothing, and much, much more.

If you're lucky enough to arrive at Schwab's when Mr. Schwab is available for a tour, you're in for a real treat. During the course of the exploration of the store, you'll hear about family reunions, the wagon yard out back at the turn of the century, the yellow fever epidemic, and other fascinating bits of Memphis history. Mr. Schwab's stories are so entertaining (with the added bonus of being "at least 10 percent true") that you'll find it as hard to leave the store as did the bus passengers about whom the driver once lamented (between gasps of laughter), "When I came in to get two people, three more got off the bus see what they had missed. Now I'm in the hole!"

- Schwab's free souvenir packet includes a pencil, a commemorative button, a postcard, and a brochure.

- Tours are informal and depend upon the availability of the inimitable Abram Schwab.

- Free parking is plentiful in the lots behind the stores on the south side of Beale Street.

- We recommend that you take a handful of nickels and pennies with you to Schwab's to try out the old weight and candy vending machines.

- Like other buildings of its age, Schwab's is not well-designed for handicapped accessibility.

- No credit cards or checks are accepted.

- Rest rooms and a water fountain are available.

Hours: Monday-Saturday, 9 a.m.-5 p.m. (Closed all day Sunday.)

Admission: FREE.

Directions: Between Second and Third Streets on Beale in downtown Memphis.

SHELBY COUNTY COURTHOUSE

140 Adams (at 2nd)
Memphis, Tennessee

Still bustling with the activity of trials, adoption finalization, research, record-keeping, and other legal endeavors almost a century after its construction, this stately government building was designed by architects H.D. Hale and J. Gamble Rogers. The building was completed in 1909.

With a grandeur befitting its image as a center for justice and the other lofty principles of the legal system, the Shelby County Courthouse has many elements of architectural beauty. Its exterior is graced by six statues representing the various virtues inherent in a just legal system. Examining the statues and discussing their significance to the laws of America could be an enlightening family activity that might go on for hours after leaving the building. The carved bust and the portrait of Andrew Jackson inside the Adams Street hallway of the building can provide another topic of interesting family discussion. The historic plaques and display cases of artifacts should not be missed.

Once the building has been explored inside and out, your family might be interested to learn more about the court system it houses. It can be fascinating to observe the legal system in action. Bailiffs posted outside the various courtrooms on the second floor of the courthouse can tell you something about the nature of the cases being tried in the courtrooms and whether the judge for a particular one would consider it proper for visitors to drop in. If allowed inside a courtroom, you must remember to be very quiet and unobtrusive — not only out of respect for the legal system itself, but also in order that the judge may hear every shred of evidence. Analysis of the court proceedings will probably be the focus of a lively conversation on your drive home. Your family might even be inspired to hold its own "moot trial" on a fabricated issue or a matter of genuine family concern.

• Metered parking is available on nearby streets.

• Vending machines are located on the first floor.

• Handicapped accessibility to the building is from the first level entrance on the north side (Washington Street).

• Rest rooms and water fountains are available.

Hours: Monday-Friday business hours.

Admission: FREE.

Directions: In the north section of downtown Memphis at the intersection of Adams and Second Streets.

SHELBY FARMS

7171 Mullins Station Road
(Administrative Office: 7161 Mullins Station Road)
Memphis, Tennessee 38134 • 382-2249

Shelby Farms is prized as "a gift from the citizens of Shelby County to themselves." Located in the heart of Shelby County, this unique urban park on 4,500 acres is the largest development of its kind in the United States. When the pastoral setting of the area was threatened by commercial development in the early 1970s, the citizens demanded that the natural beauty be preserved.

With development still in progress, Shelby Farms already is home to Agricenter International (see listing in this chapter) and an equestrian center featuring a 350-foot x 150-foot covered Showplace Arena (see listing in sports chapter), where rodeos and horse shows take place year-round. As a wildlife preserve, Shelby Farms provides a home for deer, reptiles, and other animals in quiet natural surroundings.

The land where Shelby Farms is located became in 1929 the site of the Shelby County Penal Farm, a minimum-security workhouse. The correctional facility still occupies less than 50 acres and is recognized for its model programs.

Also located within the farm are hiking, exercise, and handicap trails; picnic grounds complete with cookout grills and tables in shady nooks and under lakeside pavilions; canoe and rafting trails; fishing; an arboretum; a recreation lake designed for sailing, canoeing, and wind surfing; stables that offer horseback riding along winding trails (at hourly rental rates); and a sport shooting range with a well-supervised target area.

While you're driving through Shelby Farms, be on the lookout for the magnificent herd of American bison and Texas longhorns that roam free on the open animal range. Observe many of the 217 species of birds that inhabit the park's highlands and bottomlands. Red-tailed hawks are visible year-round. Enjoy the colorful variety of hardwood and softwood trees, apple and peach orchards. Admire the 1,000 garden plots staked out by Shelby Countians (preference going to senior citizens).

- Brochure, including a map of the farm, available at administrative office.

- Other facilities include shelters; amphitheater; picnic areas with grills; canoe, raft, and horse rentals.

- The park is handicapped accessible and offers specially designed trails for the elderly, the vision-impaired, and others with special needs.

- Rest rooms and water fountains are available at shelters.

Hours: Riding stables: daily, 8 a.m.-6 p.m. (call 382-4250). Public gun range: Wednesday-Friday, 8 a.m.-4:30 p.m.; Saturday, 10 a.m.-4 p.m.; Sunday, noon-6 p.m. (call 377-4635). Wolf River Raft Rentals (1111 Germantown Pkwy. S.): Saturday and Sunday, 9 a.m.-5 p.m. (call 365-2722).

Admission: Horseback riding: $7 per hour (300 acres to ride). Pistol/rifle range: $3 per person all day. Raft rental: $27 (includes four- to six-person raft, paddles, life jackets, and shuttle service). Group rates available.

Directions: Located in northeast Memphis. Boundaries are the Wolf River, Germantown Parkway, Raleigh LaGrange, and Mullins Station Road. If you enter through the main gate off Walnut Grove Road, you'll go directly through the park from the Wolf River to Germantown Parkway.

SPACEWALK'S FUN-PLEX

2271 Clarke Road
Memphis, Tennessee 38115 • 362-7539 or 360-8700

If you're looking for the joys of an outdoor playground inside a sheltered building, the Fun-Plex is the place to visit. Geared for even the youngest child who can walk, this complex houses a 25-foot inflated space pillow, a laser and shadow room, tunnel crawls, a giant sea of balls, and more — along with video games and even a parents' room.

This center of physical activity is a popular place to hold birthday parties, which are easily accommodated by the party rooms surrounding the activity area.

A concession stand serves food and drink.

- Children under 8 must be accompanied by an adult.

- Gift counters at entrance.

- Birthday party packages and rental of Spacewalk's are available through the Fun-Plex.

- Handicapped access available.

- Rest room and water fountain available.

Hours: Tuesday-Thursday, 10 a.m.-6 p.m. for birthday parties and special groups. Friday, noon-8 p.m.; Saturday, 10 a.m.-8 p.m.; and Sunday 1-7 p.m. for general admission, birthday parties, and special groups.

Admission: Adults, $1.35; children, $5.50. (Birthday party rates of $6.50 per child — minimum of 10 children — include use of party room for one hour, paper products, one soft drink per child, and one ice cream per child. Call 360-9000.)

Directions: Located in east Memphis off Mt. Moriah Road.

T.O. FULLER STATE PARK

1500 Mitchell Road West
Memphis, Tennessee 38109 • 543-7581 (office), 543-7771 (golf course)

T.O. Fuller State Park was one of the first four parks created by the newly-formed Department of Conservation in 1937. The State of Tennessee purchased the original 500 acres from a private citizen, Dover Barrett, and additional acquisitions have increased the park to 1,138 acres. During the excavation of a proposed swimming pool in 1940, workers unearthed evidence of a prehistoric village. The site has been developed as Chucalissa Archaeological Museum, under the management of Memphis State University. The museum lies within easy access of the park. (See separate listing in this chapter for Chucalissa.)

Renamed after Dr. Thomas Oscar Fuller (1867-1942), a Memphian and prominent minister, educator, and proponent of interracial cooperation, the park was originally called Shelby Bluffs State Park and was one of the first such havens open to African-American citizens.

The park has an 18-hole, USPGA-sanctioned golf course. Carts and clubs may be rented. Golf lessons are available through the clubhouse.

Archery enthusiasts will enjoy the regulation field course. Fourteen practice and 28 tournament targets are spread over a 20-acre range. (Fee is $2 a day per person.)

A swimming pool, centrally located in the main recreation area of the park, is equipped with a bathhouse and concession stand. The pool is open from early summer through Labor Day.

T.O. Fuller State Park offers excellent opportunities for hiking and nature walks. There is an abundance of plant and animal life, unusual in a such a small park so close to a metropolitan area. Wild turkeys, deer, horsetails, and ginseng are a few of the species to look for.

Besides a softball field and basketball and tennis courts, the park has many grassy fields for outdoor games that require open space. Children's playground equipment is located near the picnic area.

Family camping is popular at the park, which is within easy reach of the entire Memphis metropolitan area. Each of the 57 sites comes equipped with a table, grill, and hook-up and is available on a first-come, first-served basis. The centrally-located bathhouse contains personal hygiene facilities and a laundromat.

- Brochures, with a map of the park, are available.

- There are picnic tables throughout the park. Grills are available for outdoor barbecues. Pavilions may be reserved for a small fee.

- The convenient information center offers a small, interesting display of Memphis area attractions and products.

- Rest rooms and water fountains are located at pavilions and the information center.

Hours: Summer, 6 a.m.-10 p.m.; winter, 8 a.m.-sundown. Park office open Monday-Friday, 8 a.m.-4:30 p.m. (Camper quiet time begins at 10 p.m.)

Admission: There is no charge for using the natural beauty of the park. A small fee is assessed for special activities, such as archery and golf.

Directions: Located on Mitchell Road, west of U.S. Highway 61 (State Highway 14) or Third Street South, 11 miles from down town Memphis.

UNITED STATES POST OFFICE, FRONT STREET STATION

1 N. Front Street
Memphis, Tennessee 38103 • 576-2013

Built in 1885, the post office at 1 North Front Street was the first government-owned post office in Memphis and is the second oldest postal-owned building in the nation. It served as Memphis's main post office from 1885 until the new facility was built on South Third in 1972. Listed with the National Register of Historic Places, the Front Street Station still provides delivery and retail services to downtown Memphis.

It also houses administrative offices and a postal management training academy.

The low wrought-iron fence outside the post office is a wonder in itself. The curlicues and wavy spikes and spring-like adornments give it a character all its own. (If you find it fascinating, don't miss the National Ornamental Metal Museum, another downtown Memphis attraction.)

A visit at the post office could be a good time to start the hobby of philately (the collection and study of stamps). While standing in line to make the postage stamp purchase, your family might discuss the history of stamps, the efficiency of the postal service, laws governing the use of stamps, the reasons for beginning a collection, or other topics depending on the ages of the children.

- There is a very limited number of free customer angle parking spaces around the Front Street Station. Other metered spaces are available on surrounding streets.

- If you are interested in a post office tour, you might call 521-2140 for information on the availability of tours at the main post office (555 S. Third Street).

Hours: Monday-Friday, 9 a.m.-3 p.m.

Admission: FREE.

Directions: The Front Street U.S. Post Office Station is in the heart of downtown Memphis on Front Street at Madison.

VICTORIAN VILLAGE

680 Adams west to Front Street
Memphis, Tennessee

During the 1800s Memphis enjoyed prosperity and suffered through setbacks in the process of becoming a city. During this struggle of birth and growth, homes were being built by those who were shaping the city and its future. Many of these historic residences survived the hard times and are clustered together in a small area of downtown Memphis. Beautifully preserved and restored, they exemplify architecture from the neoclassical to the late Gothic revival styles.

The Woodruff-Fontaine with its magnificent displays of period antiques and Victorian clothing, the Italianate Mallory-Neely sporting many of its original furnishings, and the charming little Magevney House are three of the homes in Victorian Village. (See separate listings in this chapter for more information on each of these homes.) Another, The Massey-Shaeffer House at 664 Adams, currently houses the Memphis City Beautiful Commission.

With the exception of the houses named above, you won't be able to go inside the houses in Victorian Village, but you certainly should enjoy a self-guided walking tour. Begin at the Woodruff-Fontaine House (680 Adams) and continue west, admiring the splendor and quaint details of the houses on your route.

Tour route:
680 Adams — WOODRUFF-FONTAINE HOUSE. Built in 1870. Rear grounds are the site of the **HANDWERKER** gingerbread Queen Anne playhouse (built in 1890, moved to this location in 1973).

690 Adams — HARSON-GOYER-LEE HOUSE. 1848-1872. An example of add-on architecture, it is the "keystone" of the James Lee Memorial properties. Notice the bracketed tower, hooded windows, and keystone arch on porch.

664 Adams — MASSEY HOUSE. 1847-49. Oldest structure on the block, it survived war and the Yellow Fever epidemic. (Visitors welcome 12-1 Monday-Friday at no charge.)

662 Adams — MALLORY-NEELY HOUSE. 1852. Note the pyramidal tower roof, which was added later.

657 Adams — 1892. Building and woodwork are made of poplar.

679 Adams — TAYLOR-CARRIER HOUSE. 1886-90. This Queen Anne-style house was a wedding gift to Mollie Fontaine and W.W. Taylor from her father, Noland Fontaine.

707 Adams — PILLOW-McINTYRE HOUSE. 1852. Greek revival style. General Gideon J. Pillow is prominent among former owners. Continuing on Orleans, go south to Jefferson, then left on Jefferson to Manassas.

756 Jefferson — LOWENSTEIN HOUSE. 1891. Late Victorian using several architectural styles. Built for one of Memphis' outstanding merchants, Elias Lowenstein.

669 Jefferson and **671 Jefferson.** Restored Italianate townhouse style residences.

676 Washington — COLLINS CHAPEL CME CHURCH. 1913. The congregation's history goes back to 1859, the start of Methodism for the African American population.

102 N. Second — CALVARY EPISCOPAL CHURCH. 1844. Parish treasures include the Flemish stained-glass windows, the marble altar, and the 1935 organ.

692 Poplar — ST. MARY'S EPISCOPAL CATHEDRAL AND CHAPEL. 1857. Modified English Gothic architecture.

253 Adams — METTE-BLOUNT HOUSE. 1872. Italianate.

239 Adams — JAMES LEE SR. HOUSE. 1868. Italianate.

118 Adams — FIRE STATION #1. 1910.

128 Adams — CENTRAL POLICE STATION. 1911.

140 Adams — SHELBY COUNTY COURTHOUSE. 1909.

190 Adams — ST. PETER'S ROMAN CATHOLIC CHURCH. Gothic.

198 Adams — MAGEVNEY HOUSE. 1833. Memphis' oldest residence. Victorian.

246 Adams — TOOF-SELLERS HOUSE. 1876. Italianate.

WOODRUFF-FONTAINE HOUSE

680 Adams Avenue
Memphis, Tennessee 38103 • 526-1469

The Woodruff-Fontaine House serves as the Memphis chapter of the Association for the Preservation of Tennessee Antiquities, an organization dedicated to preserving historic properties.

Built in 1870 by Amos Woodruff and later sold to cotton factor Noland Fontaine, the home is an example of French Victorian architecture with mansard roof and *fleur de lis* trim. The Woodruff-Fontaine House is furnished with southern fine antiques and decorative items of the late 19th century.

The elaborately restored home invites children visually to enjoy life in the 19th century, noticing similarities and dissimilarities between the earlier time and their own. Antique clothing, dolls, games, books, and furniture are on display daily throughout the three-story mansion. Don't miss the Victorian Doll House.

- Brochures available.

- Visitors tour the home in guided groups. Large groups should make reservations in advance.

- Free parking available in a lot at the rear of the property.

- Children must be accompanied by adults.

- Gift shop available.

- Exhibits in the house change seasonally; Christmas season is especially popular. Victorian clothing shown on mannequins on a regular basis.

- Pre-arranged food service available for groups of 20 or more (box lunch, brunch, or dinner with tour).

- Carriage House facility available for private rental.

- First floor is handicapped accessible by ramp entry; second and third floors are not accessible to wheelchairs.

- Rest rooms available, but no water fountains.

Hours: Tours begin every half hour from 10 a.m.-3:30 p.m. Monday-Saturday and from 1-3:30 p.m. Sunday. The house is closed at 4 p.m.

Admission: Adults, $4; senior citizens and service personnel, $3; students, $2; preschoolers, free.

Directions: Seven blocks east of I-55 North off Riverside Drive. Exit Riverside Drive onto Adams Avenue. East on Adams to 680.

3. Tidbits: More Good Things To Do

C hapter 3 is, in many ways, a continuation of Chapter 2. Just as the second chapter described major tourist attractions and activities in Memphis, so will this one describe places and events that are especially appealing to families. They are not necessarily the places that first come to mind when someone thinks of Memphis, so your familiarity with some of the attractions described in this chapter will make you a popular resource with friends who are looking for something new and exciting to do. We believe that you might even come to consider your favorite discoveries here as new major attractions in Memphis.

OFF THE BEATEN PATH

Variety is the key word to describe this first section of Chapter 3. The listings here are quite similar to the diverse ones in Chapter 2. The primary difference is that the Chapter 3 places and activities are a little more obscure, perhaps a little smaller, but certainly no less important than the ones described earlier. You'll find special classes of great interest to children; small nature hideaways; historic buildings where history continues to be made; programs promoting an understanding of and appreciation for art; and much more. Not a hodge-podge exactly, nor a catch-all, but rather an assortment of treasures to explore when you're in the mood for something a little bit different that refuses to be neatly categorized elsewhere. Ecology, nature, science, history, and politics are a few of the topics you can expect to find hidden in the listings below. We've given you tidbits of information that we expect to whet your appetite and encourage you to visit the places that perhaps might otherwise have slipped your memory, seemed unworthy of a visit, or escaped your attention altogether.

ALL ABOUT KIDS SHOW

The Parenting Center of Memphis sponsors an exciting All About Kids Show each spring (usually early spring — 1992 dates are February 29-March 1). The combination "parents'/children's convention and trade show" takes place on one weekend (all day Saturday and Sunday). At the show, families in the greater Memphis area can gather useful information on products and services (from diapers to college planning) while having fun. There is an admission fee. Exhibitors change from year to year, as does the location of the show. For more information and exact details about fees, location, or planned exhibits, call 775-7266.

AMERICAN RED CROSS

The Memphis area chapter of the American Red Cross offers a number of educational classes to children of various ages at their office (1400 Central) and at other locations, such as public libraries, Girl Scout troop meeting rooms (by special arrangement), and similar gathering spots. The **Baby-sitter** class is available to children 11 and older. The cost is $10 per student for the full-day (9 a.m.-3 p.m.) class. Baby-sitter training is offered only during the summer months. **First Aid for Little People**, available to children in kindergarten through third grade, costs $4 and is offered during the summer and on some weekends during the school year. Children ages 4-6 can take **Basic Aid Training** for a fee of $8. It is offered summers and some school year weekends. All three courses provide excellent instruction in emergency procedures and normal safety precautions. Students completing any of the courses receive an official Red Cross certification card to validate their expertise. Call 726-1690 for futher information.

ANYTOWN MEMPHIS

The National Conference of Christians and Jews sponsors annual Anytown USA summer camps for high school students. The Memphis chapter of NCCJ holds its own version of Anytown each summer at Searcy, Arkansas, a town just over 100 miles from Memphis.

The goal of the camps is to provide, in as diverse a context as possible, an ideal small community. The hope is that this positive experience will enable the participants to live successfully in an American society that also happens to be very diverse. The delegate population is selected from applications with the aim of having a total balance in terms of race and gender. An attempt is made to factor in any available ethnic groups.

The camp staff works at helping the youngsters enhance their own self-esteem while learning to respect and value those students with very

different cultural backgrounds. Leadership training is a direct benefit of the camp experience. Skits are integral to the program; sports (such as swimming, volleyball, and basketball) are incidental.

Many campers have come away from Anytown praising it as a life-changing milestone. Call Dr. Harry Moore at 327-0010 for further information.

Sessions: Camp sessions are offered on two non-consecutive weeks each summer. The 1992 camp dates are July 18-25 and August 1-8.

Fees: Each weekly session is complete and costs $150 per student. (Some scholarships are available in cases of financial need.)

CHICKASAW GARDEN LAKE
Chickasaw Parkway
Memphis, Tennessee

This public Park Commission lake, located in the heart of one of Memphis's most exclusive neighborhoods, is a scene of quiet pastoral beauty. Established in 1926, this 22-acre facility is a popular haven for those interested in such low-key activities as strolling and duck feeding. No noisy playgrounds or softball fields destroy the perfect solitude here. Enjoy tidy paths along the well-kept grounds. Remember to respect the privacy of the homeowners in the surrounding residential neighborhood. Enter from Central Avenue.

THE CRYSTAL SHRINE GROTTO
Memorial Park
5668 Poplar Avenue
Memphis, Tennessee 38119 • 767-8930

The Crystal Shrine Grotto was built in the 1930s by Mexican sculptor Dionicio Rodriquez and Memorial Park founder, E. Clovis Hinds. Located within Memorial Park Cemetery, the grotto's sculpture garden is partially visible from the park's main entrance at Poplar Avenue.

Upon entering the park and passing the three-tiered fountain and reflecting pool to the left, you should continue past the Annie Laurie Rose Garden and Wishing Chair (also constructed by the "artist-in-concrete," Rodriquez). Natural-looking objects in the shapes of boulders, wooden logs, and even a tree large enough to walk through will catch your eye. This concrete-sculptured landscape is the setting for the grotto.

The Crystal Shrine Grotto is said to be the only manufactured cave of its sort in the world. Implanted quartz crystals and natural rocks give the appearance of stalagmites and stalactites in the softly-lit chambers. Within the cave are scenes from the life of Christ.

Near the grotto is a reproduction of the Cave of Machpelah, the tomb of Abraham, Sarah, Isaac, and Jacob. Also located here is the Pool of Hebron, a re-creation of one of the celebrated pools built by King Solomon. Children are fascinated by the grotto and delight in watching the goldfish in the pool.

Water fountain and rest rooms are available at the rose garden. It is suggested that large groups call in advance (767-8930, Ext. 310).

Hours: Daily, 9 a.m.-4 p.m.

Admission: FREE.

THE DANNY THOMAS-ALSAC PAVILION
332 N. Lauderdale
Memphis, Tennessee 38105 • 522-0300

The Danny Thomas-ALSAC Pavilion, on the grounds of St. Jude Children's Research Hospital, provides audio and visual historical records of the hospital (the world's largest childhood cancer research center), the American Lebanese Syrian Associated Charities (the financial support organization for the hospital), and Danny Thomas, renowned entertainer and founder of the hospital.

The pavilion, opened in 1985, features attractive display cases in the five alcoves that encircle the rotunda and give the building a star-like shape. Highlights include a model of the St. Jude complex; a videotape of an old

"Make Room for Daddy" segment; a remarkable assortment of awards, medals, trophies, and plaques amassed by Danny Thomas and the hospital; photographs and charts describing medical research techniques; memorabilia from past ALSAC fund-raising campaigns; and the gold-anodized aluminum dome, designed after the Dome of the Rock in Jerusalem. The Pavilion's Near Eastern architecture reflects the cultural heritage of its Lebanese and Syrian benefactors.

Excellent brochures, as well as a small gift shop area (closed on Saturdays), are available just inside the Pavilion. There is also a small chapel. Rest rooms and water fountain available. Handicapped accessible. Tours are self-guided. Advance notice is required for large groups.

Hours: Monday through Friday, 10 a.m.-4 p.m.; Saturday, 11 a.m.-4 p.m. Closed Sundays and holidays.

Admission: FREE, but tax-deductible donations are welcomed.

DAVIES MANOR
9140 Davies Plantation Road
Memphis, Tennessee 38133 • 386-0715 or 386-2015

Built before 1807, Davies Manor is believed to be the oldest extant home in Shelby County. The imposing log structure was altered in 1830 and again in the 1860s, but it still stands like a proud sentinel at the end of the heavily wooded alley leading to its entrance. DAR volunteers conduct tours of the home for the Davies Manor Association, which owns and maintains the historic home. Davies family history is a focal point of the narrative. Furnishings (not necessarily from the 19th century) pointed out include the rosewood piano, "coal oil" ceiling lamp, hand-woven rugs, pie safe, quilts, feather beds (for the edification of the many children who tour the home), dressing screen, victrola, and treadle sewing machine. The house itself, with its hand-hewn beams and stairwell closets for guns and boots, is the marvelous attraction here. Rest rooms are available, but no water fountain or gift shop.

Hours: May through October: Tuesdays, 1-4 p.m.

Admission: Adults, $2; children, $1.

Directions: From Memphis, take I-40 toward Nashville. Exit at Highway 64 (Exit #18). Turn right (east). Turn left at the second Stonebridge (housing development) entrance. (There are small signs posted for Davies Manor/Hills Barn.) After passing the Stonebridge Golf Course and going over the interstate viaduct, turn left at the four-way stop sign (all street signs say Davies Plantation at this intersection). By the immediate grove of trees, Davies Manor driveway will be marked with a sign on the right.

EARTH COMPLEX
Located at the end of Mitchell Road
Memphis, Tennessee 38109 • 576-6720

You can view a variety of agricultural crops, depending on the time of year, from sunflower fields (blooming in July), to pumpkin patches (picked in October), to cotton fields and sod plots. Founded as a unique concept to meet the solid waste and sludge disposal needs of the future in an environmentally sound manner, the complex is becoming a model for cities all over the United States.

One of the main attractions of the complex is the bird sanctuary. The shallow sludge lagoons and wetland areas have become a haven for a wide variety of birds, some never before seen in this area. The black-necked stilt, with its colorful orange legs, has begun nesting in this area. Bird watchers from as far as 500 miles away are attracted to this site to observe this and other birds nesting. The best months for viewing are April, May, June, September, and October. The shallow lagoons are located within the complex and are best found by following Buoy Road to the left, past the compost area. Bird crossing signs will help you locate the best vantage points.

A wilderness and wildlife reserve is also part of the complex. Hiking trails are marked, but this is "real" wilderness, complete with deer and wild turkey. It is advised to call ahead for a tour of this area.

Of particular interest to children are the Earth Day activities held in April and the Fall Festival, where kids can pick their own pumpkins, in October.

Hours: Open daily.

Directions: To find your way to this one-of-a-kind Environmental And Resource TecHnology **Complex,** just follow the directions to Chucalissa Archaeological Museum. When you pass the museum entrance to the left, stay on Mitchell Road until you see the Hugh Allen Generating Plant. The **EARTH Complex** will be on your left before you reach the steam plant.

EARTH DAY

Celebrated at the end of April each year, Earth Day has become an important opportunity to discuss conservation, recycling, and ecological issues of pollution. Festivals, workshops, lectures, and demonstrations are held around town each year around Earth Day. All members of the family are invited to attend and participate. Whether you pick up trash in your neighborhood or volunteer to help at one of the festivals, everyone needs to work together to celebrate and protect our earth. The EARTH Complex (see separate listing above) usually holds special programs or festivals to bring attention to the importance of Earth Day. All events are advertised in advance in *The Commercial Appeal,* and local libraries feature information of interest on the subject throughout the month.

ELMWOOD CEMETERY
824 S. Dudley
Memphis, Tennessee 38104 • 774-3212

Founded in 1852, Elmwood is Memphis's oldest still-active cemetery. (There are more than 20,000 lots still available, and the big 19th-century bell next to the gate cottage still tolls on the occasion of a burial at the cemetery.) The original 40 acres at the founding of Elmwood were doubled by another 40-acre purchase after the Yellow Fever Epidemic of the late 19th century obliterated much of Memphis's population, filling many of the gravesites.

Just past the little bridge at the entrance to the cemetery sits the quaint Victorian cottage built in 1866 as a superintendent's office. Helpful office staff inside gladly offer brochures and maps and volunteer interesting tidbits on the history of the cemetery. A walking tour booklet identifies the flora growing in the park-like cemetery. Another pamphlet marks the location of the graves of famous Tennesseeans.

The quiet beauty of the cemetery speaks of a simpler time in our city's past. Angels, Grecian columns, and hewn tree trunks serve as monuments to those buried beneath the grassy knolls.

Tombstone rubbings, in this or any old cemetery, can provide an entertaining diversion for a family. Use high-quality news pad paper and #3 lithographic crayons for best results. Have one person hold the paper firmly in place over the design or letters to be impressed while another person rubs lightly over the surface of the paper with the SIDE of the crayon until the design is visible. Be very careful not to tear the paper or let the crayon stray off the edge of the paper. Crayon marks on cemetery markers would be a desecration of personal property, as well as an insult to a remnant of our collective past.

For a brief look at the entire cemetery, follow Grand Tour, which makes a big loop around the grounds.

Hours: The cemetery is open from 8 a.m. till 5 p.m. daily. (The office is open 8 a.m.-4 p.m. Monday-Friday.)

Admission: FREE.

Directions: Reach Elmwood Cemetery by driving south on Dudley Street until it ends with the little bridge at the entrance.

MEMPHIS COLLEGE OF ART SATURDAY SCHOOL
Overton Park
Memphis, Tennessee 38112 • 726-4085

The Memphis College of Art offers an extensive array of classes and workshops for children as young as 2 1/2. Included in the curriculum are drawing and painting, photography, pottery, computer graphics, printmaking, and sculpture. During the school year the Saturday school is a popular outlet for the creative young mind. Shows featuring students' works are offered periodically during the year in the gallery at the college. Comparable summer classes are available. (See Memphis College of Art listing in the art gallery section of Chapter 2 for additional information.)

MEMPHIS COTTON EXCHANGE AND COTTON ROW
92 South Front Street
Memphis, Tennessee 38103 • 525-3361

The twelve-story Memphis Cotton Exchange building once handled one-third of all cotton traded in the United States. Modern methods of trading in corporate offices over telephone lines and computer screens have left the Cotton Exchange using only the first two floors of the building. These two floors house small offices, lounges, and meeting rooms for the cotton merchants.

Cotton was first traded in Memphis in 1826 with the delivery of 300 pounds of cotton. Selling price was 10 cents a pound! By 1840, 35,000 bales of cotton were traded by some 26 buyers. Receipts totaling $39,552,000 were recorded in 1870 for approximately 400,000 bales. To set standards and promote cotton, the Memphis Cotton Exchange was formed in 1874. The Exchange has occupied several grand buildings, but the cotton business has always been located along Front Street. The words of W.J. Britton describe Front Street's good times and bad on a bronze plaque located on the northwest corner of the Cotton Exchange building.

Front Street is lined with buildings that once were headquarters to cotton merchants. Although some of these buildings are now condominiums, the large windows and north-facing clear stories and skylights that were used for classing cotton are still visible today. When Front Street, between Beale and Monroe, is viewed from adjacent high-rise offices, the clear stories and skylights abound.

This area on Front Street originally became the hub of the cotton business because of its proximity to the Wolf and Mississippi Rivers. Flatboats and steamboats would unload on the cobblestones, and ox-carts would haul the heavy wagons up the steep bluff. Before moving on to warehouses, the cotton was piled high along Front, creating a tall corridor. Today cotton bales can still be seen on the street, but these are only scattered bales of cotton formed from discarded trays of cotton samples. (While standing on the cobblestones by the river and looking up towards Front Street, you can get a real sense of what life must have been like long ago.)

There is very little trading on the Memphis Cotton Exchange today, but much of the history is still there to be seen. A visit to the **Carter Seed Store,** located on Front across the street from the Cotton Exchange, can almost take you back in time. You might even leave with a small "pocket-sized" bale of cotton purchased as a souvenir of days gone by.

MEMPHIS IN MAY INTERNATIONAL FESTIVAL
245 Wagner Place, Suite 220
Memphis, Tennessee 38103 • Hotline: 684-2639

Although this festival is listed in our chapter "Festivals and Special Events," the month-long celebration is such a major event in Memphis that it requires more space than the thumbnail sketch allotted to entries in the calendar-like chapter. This month-long tidbit is one that you must not miss. Several official events take place under the umbrella of Memphis in May, with people from all over the world participating.

Each year a country is chosen to be the "celebrant." Past festivals have honored Egypt, Japan, Spain, Venezuela, Israel, China, Africa, Australia, England, and others. In 1992 the celebrated country will be Italy. The Memphis in May committee brings in cultural activities such as art exhibits and performing artists from the prominent country and hosts a variety of annual events that promote not only the honored country but also the city of Memphis. _The Commercial Appeal_ and other news sources often run educational series or create special pieces on the honored country. Local schools also become involved in the education process. We have outlined below several annual events, each occurring in May.

MIM Barbecue Contest — listed in the _1990 Guinness Book of World Records_ as the largest of its kind in the world. Featuring over 150 teams preparing pork barbecue to perfection and trying to become "Grand Champion." The Hog Calling Contest, Porker Promenade, and Showmanship Competition are "extras" during the weekend of cooking.

MIM Triathlon — ranks in the top ten in the country. Includes a 1.5K (approximately one mile) swim, 25-mile bike race, and 10K (six-mile) run. Held in Meeman-Shelby State Park.

Great Mississippi Canoe and Kayak Race — a three-mile race down the Mississippi River finishing at the Memphis Harbor. The largest race of its kind in the southeastern United States.

MIM Beale Street Music Festival — a weekend of blues, rock 'n' roll, rhythm and blues, and rockabilly.

Great Wine Race — as much fun for spectators as for the contestants. Four-member relay teams from participating restaurants compete in uncorking, pouring, and carrying their bottle of wine 100 yards while clearing a hurdle. Spilling the wine is a no-no, costing the team coveted points.

Kids Fest — held at Libertyland. This "Mini Memphis in May" includes puppet shows, singers, storytellers, mimes, crafts, and magicians.

Sunset Symphony — the grand finale of the whole month. Signifying the end of the festival, this outdoor concert on the banks of the Mississippi River is one of the most popular events of the year in Memphis. Picnickers spend the day waiting at their staked-out, quilt-covered spot for the main event. The Memphis Symphony Orchestra plays a variety of musical pieces, with the highlight being "The 1812 Overture," complete with cannons, and James Hyter's rendition of "Ol' Man River." An explosion of fireworks over the Mississippi River wraps up the concert and the Memphis in May festival for the year.

Several additional events are planned within the month by local shops and restaurants. There is no lack of food or fun, so be sure to keep abreast of all the events. *The Commercial Appeal* lists schedules well in advance, and the Memphis in May committee publishes a brochure listing all events in and around the city.

MIFA CITY CAMP
MIFA's Center for Neighborhoods
619 North Seventh Street
Memphis, Tennessee 38107 • 527-6627

Sponsored by the Metropolitan Interfaith Association, City Camp is a unique opportunity awaiting young people ages 12 to 14. Every effort is made to select a group of adolescents who will be representative of the diversity of Memphis. The camp involves sharing, working, and playing, in addition to discussing the quality of life in Memphis. The week-long camp includes a day spent delivering meals to the elderly for the Home-Delivered Meals program, a day visiting the courts, and another day helping build a home for a family in need. Each participant is given an opportunity to learn, grow, and make new friends.

Campers should bring sack lunches unless otherwise informed. Limited scholarships are available, and registration is limited.

Hours: The camp runs from a Sunday through a Friday, with most days lasting from 9 a.m. until 3 p.m. (There is one overnight session during the week.)

MUSEUM SCOPE-THE PINK PALACE MUSEUM
3050 Central Avenue
Memphis, Tennessee 38111 • 320-6320

The Memphis Pink Palace Museum offers a wide range of workshops and classes for kids from 4-year-olds to fourth-graders. Topics might include dinosaurs — how and when they lived and died; fossils — hands-on examination of what a fossil is and where to find one; earthquakes — what makes them happen; planets and our solar system — examining the bigger world we live in; or insects — a close look at nature's tiny creatures. Class topics vary according to age. These classes fill up fast, so call early for schedules and reservations.

Hours: During the school year classes are held on Saturday morning; summer schedules are week-long sessions.

NURSERIES

Visiting a nursery and enjoying the rows and rows of all kinds of flowering plants, bushes with assorted shapes, bundled roots at the base of a tree, and grasses cut in squares is a lively activity for even the littlest city slicker. For a small investment (usually less than $1), a parent can lead a toddler into the world of science. Elementary-aged children might spend allowance money on a carefully chosen plant for their room — a venture that can be as much fun as picking out a new pet. A summer project might include planning a small garden and researching what plants will grow best in your available space. Every season brings a new variety of pleasures, so be sure to schedule a visit during each one. A wide selection of *Nurseries* is listed in the Yellow Pages.

A family trip to an area Christmas Tree Farm is one of our favorite annual events. Everyone sets aside one afternoon during the busy holiday season to sing carols on the way to one of the farms on the outskirts of town. **Santa's Forest**, with owner "Christmas Tree Larry," and **Fite Road Christmas Trees** are both located out Highway 51 toward Millington. Look for the signs directing you to either site. Open from Thanksgiving until Christmas Eve, each has unique offerings and provides everything you need to chop down your holiday tree.

OVERTON SQUARE
24 South Cooper Street
(extending south on Cooper and west on Madison)
Memphis, Tennessee 38104 • 274-0671 or 726-0025

A favorite of families, Overton Square is located in the very heart of midtown Memphis. This landmark district offers a few specialty shops. Several architectural styles are present, including bungalow residential buildings, turn-of-the-century storefronts, and more current structures scattered about.

A walk down the sidewalks will really get your mouth watering. Whatever you're hankering for, the "Square" is sure to have some of the best. Mexican burritos, Cajun red beans and rice, Greek baklava, French crepes, Oriental delicacies, together with American burgers and Memphis barbecued ribs, are just a few of the menu items waiting for you at the numerous restaurants here.

The shops are a child's delight. Small enough not to overwhelm, each has selected items that would intrigue any youngster. In its heyday, Overton Square had a wonderful diversity of shops. Many of the shops have closed in past years, but the Square has seen a renewal of interest in recent months that should restore life to the vacant space and bring neighbors to the toy, magazine, holiday, and other shops that have survived.

Summer months on the square might include weekend visits by Teardrop the Clown with imaginative balloon sculptures for kids. Holiday activities include Christmas visits by Dickens characters singing carols and vendors selling hot roasted chestnuts against a backdrop of thousands of twinkling lights outlining each storefront and every tree branch.

In case mom and dad would like a night out to themselves, Overton Square has everything from live music (jazz to classical) performed on restaurant patios . . . to a comedy club filled with laughter (and occasional special shows just for children) . . . to a live theatre presenting a wide repertoire of stage plays (many suitable for the entire family). Kids and all will enjoy the popular "Celebration on the Square: From Bach to Rock" held each fall at Overton Square.

PLEASURABLE PLAYGROUNDS

We felt obliged to enter a paragraph or two on great Memphis-area playgrounds. Young and old, we all love a good playground. Free to everyone, these specially designed "have-a-great-time" play areas with their swings, slides, and climbing structures bring out the child in all of us. Memphis bubbles over with innumerable delightful playgrounds. Here are a few to get you started on your own best-playgrounds search:

Audubon Park Playground — west side of park, near pavilion.

Avon Park — 310 Avon

Cameron Brown Park — east end of Farmington Rd. in Germantown.

Evergreen Presbyterian Church — Tutwiler at University.

Grace St. Luke's/Central Gardens Playground — Central Avenue (available weekends and after school).

Overton Park — adjacent to Rainbow Lake.

Remember to check the safety of any playground before releasing your child to cut loose and have fun. Make sure the equipment is properly sized for your child. All equipment should be firmly and securely planted in the ground. Check metal surfaces, such as slides and swings, in the hot sun to make sure they will not burn your child's sensitive skin. The ground surface of the playing area should provide cushioning for pounding feet and tumbling bodies: pea gravel, wood chips, and rubber are acceptable surfaces. Watch for openings that could trap heads.

Kids can't get enough of playgrounds, so take them often to their favorite spots, and join in on the fun yourself.

PUDDLEJUMPERS
Lichterman Nature Center
5992 Quince Road
Memphis, Tennessee 38119 • 767-7322

Just like its home — Lichterman Nature Center — Puddlejumpers is a wonderfully unique part of the Memphis landscape. The nine-month program (September-May) is designed for 4-year-olds who register for the entire course and attend every Monday and Wednesday from 9 a.m. till noon. With an emphasis on nature, activities lead to a better understanding of such topics as ecology, life cycles, and relationships between plants and animals. Enjoying outside time and interaction with the world around them, children experience a wide variety of stimulating situations. To be eligible to register, all class members must have their 4th birthday by October 1. Lichterman also offers **Summer Ecology Camps** for preschoolers through sixth-graders.

RECYCLING

Everyone is now aware of the essential nature of recycling. Conserving natural resources to enhance the quality of our environment is no longer the trendy pastime it might have been at one time — it is now a necessity for the continuation of life as we know it. Our future, and especially our children's future, depends on our ability and willingness to take the time to return to the earth what rightfully belongs to it.

Curbside recycling has recently been implemented in some Memphis neighborhoods, with the promise that it will eventually spread all over the city. Schools and youth organizations have paper drives, and everyone seems to have a bag of aluminum cans tucked away in a closet, awaiting a trip to the recycling bins.

Children not only realize the importance of recycling, but also have a great time participating. They are taking an active role in their future, and as parents we need to encourage them and show good examples ourselves.

Area grocery stores have depositories for cans, newspapers, and plastic. Many encourage shoppers to reuse their grocery sacks by taking cents off their shopping bill for each returned bag. The EARTH Complex (see separate listing in this section of Chapter 3) is an excellent source of information on what is being done in our community.

SUN RECORD STUDIO
706 Union Avenue
Memphis, Tennessee 38103 • 521-0664

A must for Elvis Presley aficionados, Sun Record Studio is the historic spot where Sam Phillips discovered the King of Rock 'n' Roll in 1953. The colorful narrative that makes up the tour of the one-room studio highlights Elvis's career and adds anecdotes about other famous musicians who have recorded at Sun Studio.

Excerpts from recording sessions include selections from Ike Turner, Rufus Thomas, Charlie Rich, Jerry Lee Lewis, and others. The history of the studio is traced from its beginnings in the early '50s to the present, a time when international stars still bring their talents in to cut a label.

Musical instruments and equipment on display in the studio (and actually used during recording sessions) include drums, a piano, guitars, amplifiers, and microphones. The old WHBQ microphone used by Dewey Phillips is the showpiece.

Tickets for the studio tour are purchased in the adjoining Sun Studio Cafe, which features an exact reissue of a 1949 Wurlitzer jukebox — a real classic. Upstairs is a gift shop which offers T-shirts, guitar picks, records, and other music-oriented souvenirs.

Hours: Daily. Studio offers guided half-hour tours every hour on the half-hour from 9:30 a.m.-8:30 p.m., June-August and from 10:30 a.m.-5:30 p.m. September-May.

Admission: Adults, $4; children 4-12, $3; children under 4, free. Group rates are available.

Directions: The studio is located just seven blocks east of the Mississippi River on Union Avenue. (Free parking in the rear.)

THEATRE CONSERVATORY
Playhouse on the Square
51 S. Cooper
Memphis, Tennessee

Circuit Playhouse
1705 Poplar Avenue
Memphis, Tennessee • 726-4656

Two midtown Memphis professional acting companies offer a summer conservatory for young thespians. The junior conservatory for children aged 6-11 has two two-week sessions; the senior conservatory for ages 12-17 offers two three-week sessions. The training is then exhibited in a public production at the end of the second session. All juniors get to participate; seniors must audition for roles. There is a fee for students. Call either theatre for more information on the conservatory or the other summer and school-year weekly classes offered to youth and adults.

WAPANOCCA NATIONAL WILDLIFE REFUGE
Box 279
Turrell, Arkansas 72384 • 501-343-2595

Wapanocca National Wildlife Refuge is located about 30 minutes northwest of Memphis on the Arkansas side of the Mississippi River. The refuge offers visitors a close-up, undisturbed view of nature. Catch a glimpse of some of the native wildlife, including deer and opossum. Hawks can be seen in the fall, and if you're lucky November is the month when the American bald eagle might make a stop or two in the area. A small museum includes a display of regional animals. While you're there, pick up the map directing you around the seven-mile nature drive. Kids find this a great getaway from the city without having to travel for hours.

Hours: Daylight to dark, with the office open weekdays 8 a.m.-4:30 p.m.

Directions: Take I-40 across the Hernando de Soto Bridge. Go north on Highway 77 to the Turrell exit. Signs lead the way from here.

WONDERS: THE MEMPHIS INTERNATIONAL CULTURAL SERIES
Memphis Cook Convention Center
255 N. Main
Memphis, Tennessee 38103 • 576-1200

The first installment in the city's Wonders International Cultural Series was the widely acclaimed 1991 Catherine the Great Exhibition, showing magnificent treasures for the first time outside the Soviet Union. More than 600,000 visitors came from all over the United States to see the priceless art objects from imperial Russia—costumes, jewelry, Catherine's coronation coach, and much more.

The series exhibitions planned by the city of Memphis for the future promise to be just as exciting as the first one. 1992 will bring to Memphis "Splendors of the Ottoman Sultans" and a show of Etruscan artifacts. (Some local museums are planning to offer companion shows, just as they did in 1991 for the Russian exhibition.) A Napoleon exhibition (touted to be the greatest one ever) is scheduled for 1993. If negotiations go well, Memphians can expect to see an exhibition from the People's Republic of China in 1994.

This cultural art series, besides being a major attraction for tourists from hundreds of miles away, provides an excellent opportunity for local residents to enjoy the beauty and wonder of art treasures from around the world and to learn more about the people who live in the lands where the artwork originated.

ZOO CAMP
Memphis Zoo and Aquarium
Overton Park
Memphis, Tennessee 38112 •725-4768 (Education Dept.)
or 726-4775 (Zoo Information)

Every child dreams of the opportunity to get closer to and learn more about the exotic animals in the zoo. Dreams come true for those youngsters attending the Zoo Camp hosted by the Memphis Zoo and Aquarium. Elementary students entering grades one through five are divided by grade. They experience firsthand what it is like to be a zookeeper. Session titles have included: "Hide 'n' Seek" (natural camouflage), "If I Ran the Zoo" (zookeeping), and "Where in the World" (habitats). Some hands-on instruction, along with behind-the-scenes observations, is included together with arts and crafts projects, stories, and other forms of instruction.

The camp is held each summer. Campers should remember to bring water and wear a hat: Memphis summers can be rather hot and humid. Campers also should bring their own lunch. These sessions fill up fast, and members of the Memphis Zoological Society get first choice of sessions, so watch for details and call early.

Hours: 9 a.m.-2.p.m.

FARMER'S MARKETS
AND
PICK YOUR OWN

——— FARMER'S MARKETS ———

Food shopping is an inescapable task. Whether you enjoy clipping coupons and gliding down the aisles of a supermarket or really detest the weekly undertaking, you — or someone in the family — must buy food regularly. After all, human beings have to eat. Food shopping can be livelier than the routine trip to the large chain food store. When time is in such supply that the one-stop convenience of the supermarket is not demanded, small meat markets and fish markets, colorful flower markets, aromatic bakeries, and other specialty shops can turn into a pleasurable outing for shoppers and their pint-sized assistants. Listed below are a few spots offering an impressive array of fresh fruits and vegetables. Many smaller open-air markets are open seasonally. Look for your own favorite spots for home-grown vegetables, as well as locations to find the other items on your weekly grocery list.

Scott Street Market: Shelby County Growers Association
814 Scott Street
Memphis, Tennessee 38112 • 327-8828

Farm-fresh fruits and vegetables from the surrounding area converge at this open-air market. Depending on the growing season, you might find truckloads of apples, bushels of tomatos, pints of strawberries, or bins of vegetables. While wandering through the market you may decide to pick out a basket of cucumbers and try your hand at pickling or pick out some area fruit and "put up" jars of jam. Many growers also bring along homemade relishes, pickled vegetables, and sorghum molasses. Hours: Monday-Saturday from 4 a.m. to 7 p.m. and Sunday from 8 a.m. to 6 p.m.

Collierville Town Square Farmer's Market
Rowlett Street on Historic Town Square

You're likely to find anything from pumpkins, peas, and peppers to carrots, corn, and cantaloupe along this shady stretch of the historic town square. Check for farmers on weekdays of the growing season.

Farmer's Market at Agricenter
7777 Walnut Grove Road
Memphis, Tennessee • 756-4247

Open 7 a.m.-6 p.m. Monday-Saturday, year-round.

Easy Way Food Stores
596 S. Cooper • 726-4917
337 N. Cleveland • 725-6889
4599 Elvis Presley Boulevard • 345-6519
80 N. Main • 523-1323
814 Mt. Moriah Road • 683-8249
5905 Stage Road • 388-9973
5215 Winchester • 362-6620

Market Basket
4862 Summer Avenue • 682-8361

Easy Way and Market Basket are well-known enclosed markets that are like a much-enlarged fresh produce section of the supermarket. They offer a few other grocery staples, but for the most part they are big, diverse fruit and vegetable markets.

PICK YOUR OWN FOOD

Even better than the fruit and vegetable market is the countryside farm, orchard, or vineyard that allows customers to pick their own produce. Nothing in a store can offer the juicy tang of a morsel pulled right off its vine. Our modern, urban conveniences have deprived us of the pleasure of running out to the vegetable garden or "truck patch" to gather each day's meal just before preparing it. But an occasional trip to a nearby commercial farm leaves the family with a feeling of appreciation for their food sources and gratification for the simple task of gathering their own food from the land and consuming it while it is still bursting with flavor. Call ahead before visiting the farms in Shelby and other nearby counties listed below to determine what produce is in season — if any. Even city slickers shouldn't expect to pick fresh blackberries in January! Also check to find out whether you'll be allowed to pick your own food and what harvesting equipment you'll need to bring with you.

SHELBY COUNTY:

Briscoe's Table Grapes
4265 Sykes Road
Millington, Tennessee 38053 • 872-2071

Gragg Farms
8780 Gragg Road
Millington, Tennessee 38053 • 829-3467

Harrell Vineyard & Berry Farm
8745 Jack Bond Road
Arlington, Tennessee 38002 • 829-3148

Harris Farms
7521 Sledge Road
Millington, Tennessee 38053 • 872-0696

Jones Orchard
5762 Pleasant Ridge Road
Millington, Tennessee 38053 • 872-0383

Leggett's Pick Your Own Strawberry Farm
8143 Austin Peay Highway
Millington, Tennessee 38053 • 829-3402

TIPTON COUNTY:

Goforth Orchard
4139 Holly Grove Road
Covington, Tennessee 38019 • 476-7598

LAUDERDALE COUNTY:

Hughes Produce Farm
Route 3, Box 209A
Ripley, Tennessee 38063 • 635-4613

Jimmie Summar Farm
Route 5, Box 121
Ripley, Tennessee 38063 • 635-5405

Mike Voss Farms
Route 3
Ripley, Tennessee 38063 • 635-0739

Prater Farms
Route 4, Box 100B
Ripley, Tennessee 38063 • 635-8632

R & H Farms
Route 4
Ripley, Tennessee 38063 • 635-1674

HARDEMAN COUNTY:

Anderson Fruit Farm
Route 1, Box 115,
Toone, Tennessee 38381

Second location:
Hwy. 45
S. Jackson • 658-5524

HAYWOOD COUNTY:

Mooreland Plantation
1155 Sewanee Road
Nashville, Tennessee 37220
(Located seven miles west of Brownsville, Hwy. 54 • 772-0707)

Norris Strawberry Farm
Route 3
Bells, Tennessee 38006 • 772-4320

Oswald Orchards
4961 Highway 70 West
Brownsville, Tennessee 38012 • 772-9786

STORYTELLING, LIBRARIES, AND BOOKSTORES

STORYTELLING

Storytelling, the central leisure-time occupation of our ancestors, has just about gone the way of taffy-pulls, hayrides, and barn raisings, other sources of enjoyment for our grandparents. Although few of us would like to return to the hard labor and difficult times of an earlier age, we would do well to recognize the losses we have suffered by letting modern conveniences obliterate the past — the good as well as the bad. Plugging in to a video monitor or TV screen can't hold a light to sitting down with someone a couple of generations older and wiser and hearing firsthand accounts of that person's life experiences. A good storyteller's tale — whether tall or circumspect — allows the listener to become involved in the episode being recounted. The imagination can run wild; flights of fancy create a joy unequaled by canned laughter or any other element of electronic transmission.

Not quite extinct yet and enjoying a resurgence of interest on the national level, storytelling can excite in your child a sense of wonder and pleasure surpassing even the delights of being read aloud to. If you don't know any good storytellers (but don't be surprised to find that you are skilled yourself once you get going!), try the bookstores and library programs listed below. Also, the next time your family visits with your own parents, ask an innocent question like "What do you remember about *your* grandfather?" or "How did you two meet?" or "What was the funniest thing that ever happened in your elementary school?", and see where things go from there. Parents and grandparents who have some amusing bits of family lore to share are usually the most spellbinding of storytellers. *Our* children can sit for hours at their grandparents' sides, rolling with laughter about the humorous pranks their own parents' *parents* pulled on their friends and teachers or crying over the dramatic accounts of hard times in the Depression. Be ready to participate yourself in the lively conversation that is likely to ensue. After all, storytelling and sharing of family folklore can create a genuine bond for families as well as provide them with wonderful entertainment.

Professional storytellers are often on the staff of public libraries, usually employed in the children's department; others are featured by bookstores that cater exclusively to children or that offer large, impressive children's book sections. These experienced tellers of tales will combine story, drama, personal presence, sometimes audience participation, and occasionally music or props such as puppets to create a thoroughly delightful amusement for parents and children alike.

There are a few affiliations around town for storytellers and wanna-be's. The children's department at the main library can put you in touch with **Yarn Spinners**, an association of people interested in promoting and learning more about storytelling. **Delta Rising** is a group of storytelling performers who participate in festivals such as Arts in the Park and also occasionally entertain at such events as children's birthday parties. Call 278-1768 for more information. Other groups around town include the **Storytellers League of Memphis** and **Tennessee Association for the Preservation and Perpetuation of Storytelling.**

LIBRARIES

One of the first outings children are likely to remember is a trip to the library. Memphis/Shelby County Public Library and Information Center schedules an enormous number of programs for children of all ages. Materials available at the library include not only thousands of marvelous books, records, and tapes, but a vast assortment of exceptional activities as well.

For the youngest child (ages 2-5) there is **Toddler Story Time**, held weekly at most branches. The main library on Peabody also has the popular **Pajama Powwow** one night a week, where kids come "almost ready for bed" and cuddle up to listen to a storyteller. Many branches also have a weekly film series for all ages, usually held after school hours.

Puppet shows, arts and crafts classes, babysitting workshops, and the popular **Summer Reading Program** are just a handful of the activities waiting for kids.

While your children are enjoying all the impressive programs, you can look into what is available for parents. Discussion groups, parenting lectures, and educational workshops are offered periodically. Brochures on a variety of subjects from area bus schedules to health care services are available at the Information Desk.

With more than 20 branch locations, the public library system is sure to offer services close to your own home. Call the branch nearest you to find out what is offered there. The libraries are listed in the Blue Pages of the phone book under **Memphis City Government — Public Library.** Pick up a copy (available at all branches) of _Kaleidoscope_, the library's monthly calendar/newsletter which lists upcoming events for all locations. The **main library** is located at 1850 Peabody Avenue, Memphis, Tennessee 38104 (725-8801). The number for the Children's Department is 725-8819.

BOOKSTORES

Saturday morning is the time to take advantage of free programs offered by local bookstores for family entertainment. **Choo-Choo Children's Books and Toys** at 4615-14 Poplar (761-5366) features "Choo-Choo's Platform" each Saturday at 10:30 a.m. The weekly presentations are designed for children and their families — to inform and entertain. Storytelling is one of many types of programs; other Saturday morning features include art projects, visits by career professionals, storybook characters, plays, and cooking classes. (A similar summer series is available to pre-registered participants for a fee.)

Davis-Kidd Booksellers Inc. at 397 Perkins Road Ext. (683-9801) offers all kinds of wonderful programs for adults as well as families and children. The regular Saturday morning children's programs at Davis-Kidd take place at 11 a.m. from January through November. Storytelling is a standard feature of this series. The bookstore has brought storytellers into town for the programs and sometimes features children's authors. For more information on upcoming events, pick up Davis-Kidd's own newsletter and calendars, available just inside the front door of the store, or check newspaper listings. (Davis-Kidd also joins in the local literacy efforts in such ways as sponsoring a project to provide books to homeless children.)

"Super Saturdays" is the name for the series offered by **Only Kids** at 6150 Poplar Avenue (683-1234). Activities for children and their parents include storytelling and crafts. The great toys/clothes/books store also offers a Halloween party, an Easter egg hunt, and other holiday celebrations.

The Deliberate Literate at 206 N. Evergreen (276-0174) is a fairly new elegant little bookstore that has worked hard to build up a good children's section. Monthly art and literature programs, such as origami workshops and chalk drawing experiments and storytelling, are one way the store is generating interest in stories and books. Call for more information.

Other bookstores that offer occasional programs of interest to children, including storytelling, are **Pinocchio's Children's Book Store** at 688 W. Brookhaven Circle (767-6586) and **The Booksmith** at 3092 Poplar (323-4021). Watch the newspaper for special listings.

TOURS OF THE WORKING WORLD

Even young children who know little about the "working world" beyond the tasks of teachers, doctors, and clerks are fascinated by the equipment, uniforms, ID badges, safety goggles, assembly lines, and other paraphernalia of the various sites of business and industry. A number of civic-minded companies and public service organizations in the Memphis area are happy to invite families into their facilities for an up-close view of how their plants operate. Your child might even discover a future career goal while learning the technical aspects of how machines work.

ALLEN GENERATING PLANT
Steam Plant Road
Memphis, Tennessee 38109 • 785-7490

Children of all ages may take a tour to see how electricity is generated. Follow the step-by-step process from the boiler rooms to the observation window overlooking the powerful turbines making electricity.

Tours: Call in advance between 9 a.m. and 4 p.m. for an appointment.

Admission: FREE.

Directions: Allen Generating Plant is located across the way from the EARTH Complex.

CENTER FOR EARTHQUAKE RESEARCH AND INFORMATION
3890 Central Avenue
Memphis, Tennessee 38152 • 678-2007

The tour of this unique facility, which is guided by graduate students from Memphis State University, includes a film about earthquakes, a question-and-answer opportunity, and a walking tour through the actual rooms where the huge drums (seismographs) are recording earth tremors and quakes and the computers are printing out pertinent information.

Tours: Geared for children ages 6 and up, the tour takes about an hour. The maximum size of a group is between 25 and 30 children. Tours are available on Tuesdays and Thursdays. Call in advance for a reservation.

Admission: FREE.

CHANNEL 5 WMC-TV AND RADIO FM 100
1960 Union Avenue
Memphis, Tennessee 38104 • 726-0555

Visit two studios and the newsroom; then peek at the control room on this popular TV tour. Children in seventh grade and above are led through the station and encouraged to ask questions and learn the ropes of broadcast media.

Tours: The tour can last from 15 to 45 minutes, depending on breaking news and studio time, so be prepared. The maximum size for a group is 30 children. You must make reservations in advance.

Admission: FREE.

COLONIAL BAKING COMPANY
1340 Larkin Avenue
Memphis, Tennessee 38104 • 726-9104

Take a guided tour through the production plant of this large bakery to observe the bread-making process. Watch the dough being mixed and readied for baking, and see the ovens where thousands of loaves of bread march in and out. Slicing and wrapping are the last stops on the tour (and if you're lucky you might get a little treat at the end).

Tours: The tours are for children ages 5 and up and last between 45 minutes and an hour. Group size is limited to 45 children. One tour a day is scheduled for Wednesdays and Thursdays, usually in mid-morning (around 10 a.m.). Call ahead to reserve your tour.

Admission: FREE.

THE COMMERCIAL APPEAL
495 Union Avenue
Memphis, Tennessee 38103 • 529-2241

This one-hour tour begins with a film containing information on the history of the newspaper. A walking tour of the facility takes you past the typesetters and the bustling newsroom.

Tours: The tour is appropriate for children ages 10 and older, with a limit of 20 to a group. (Two groups may tour simultaneously.) Schedule your tours well in advance.

Admission: FREE.

CORDOVA CELLARS
9050 Macon Road
Cordova, Tennessee 38018 • 754-3442

Tours of the winery and commercial vineyard are available. See listing in Chapter 1 for more information.

COORS MEMPHIS BELLE
5151 East Raines Road
Memphis, Tennessee 38118 • 375-2100

Walk through the step-by-step process of beer manufacturing and bottling, and watch the huge conveyor systems through the observation windows. Refreshments are offered in the hospitality room, which is designed like a riverboat.

Tours: Tour the brewery Monday-Saturday from 10 a.m. till 4 p.m. Groups should call in advance for a tour.

Admission: FREE.

EARTH COMPLEX
Located at the end of Mitchell Road
Memphis, Tennessee 38109 • 576-6720

Tours of this truly unique facility are available through advance reservations. See separate listing in the first section of this chapter for more information.

EL CHICO MEXICAN RESTAURANT
3491 Poplar Avenue
Memphis, Tennessee 38111 • 323-9609

Kids ages 5-12 love this tour. All receive a soda and a Mexican pastry along with their walk-through of the kitchen.

Tours: Best times for the tour are around 10:30 a.m. or 2 p.m., with the tour lasting about 45 minutes, depending on group size. A week or two's notice is needed for reservations.

Admission: A nominal fee of 75 cents per child is charged.

FIRE STATIONS

Your local fire station will be glad to schedule a tour of the facility. Look in the Blue Pages of the phone book under **City of Memphis, Fire Department,** for the station nearest you, and set up the fun. Included in the tour is an explanation of how the calls come in and how the firefighters get ready to answer the call. Kids love sounding the horn on the big bright red trucks.

Admission: FREE.

FITE ROAD CHRISTMAS TREE FARM
2040 Fite Road
Memphis, Tennessee • 353-4667

Open from Thanksgiving Day through Christmas Eve, the Christmas Tree Farm offers kids a hayride through acres and acres of trees. Young and old alike are delighted to witness the real, working farm, with its crop of Christmas trees.

Tours: Best times for group tours are during the week from 9 a.m. to 5 p.m. Call for a reservation.

Admission: FREE.

Directions: Take Highway 51 towards Millington. Turn left onto Fite Road and follow the signs.

KRISPY KREME DOUGHNUTS
4244 Elvis Presley Blvd.
Memphis, Tennessee 38116 • 332-0620

Tours: Watch the doughnuts being mixed, baked, and iced on Mondays or Thursdays between the hours of 1 p.m. and 3 p.m. Groups should be no larger than 25, and groups of children under 5 must have one adult with every four children. After the tour enjoy a small soft drink and a complimentary doughnut.

Admission: FREE.

LAUREL HILL VINEYARD
1370 Madison Avenue
Memphis, Tennessee 38104 • 725-9128

Tours of this Midtown estate winery are available on a drop-in basis for small groups or by arrangement for large groups. See listing in Chapter 2 for more information.

MEMPHIS INTERNATIONAL AIRPORT
2491 Winchester Road
Memphis, Tennessee

Although no "official tour" is available at the airport, families and groups are encouraged to take a self-guided tour of the area's largest airport facility. Ticket counters, baggage claim areas, and the main concourse with plenty of observation windows are the highlights of the airport adventure. Try finding the moving sidewalks, or just sit back, perhaps indulge in a soft drink from one of the many vendors, and do some serious "people watching." Pay parking is the only parking available.

MEMPHIS/SHELBY COUNTY PUBLIC LIBRARY AND INFORMATION CENTER
1850 Peabody Avenue
Memphis, Tennessee 38104 • 725-8819

Tours: The main location of the public library offers a few tours to accommodate even the youngest reader (or listener). For third-graders and younger children, a tour of the children's department is available on Tuesdays, Wednesdays, and Thursdays, preferably in the early afternoon. This 20-30 minute tour includes a short film and a walk-through of the department. Children older than third-graders receive a tour of the entire library, visiting all the departments. This tour lasts about an hour and is available on the same schedule as the tours for younger children. Reservations for tours need to be made about three to four weeks prior to your expected visit.

Admission: FREE.

MEMPHIS WATER PUMPING STATIONS
Memphis Light, Gas, and Water Division
Communication Services Department • 528-4557

Memphis is said to have some of the best water in the world. Find out how Memphis's water supply is drawn from giant natural reservoirs deep in the earth. Nine water pumping plants operated by Memphis Light, Gas, and Water Division supply water to the city and some adjacent areas of Shelby County.

Tours: Call to arrange a tour of any of the nine stations located throughout the city. Tours are given Monday through Friday, and all groups are welcome.

Admission: FREE.

NATIONAL WEATHER SERVICE
7777 Walnut Grove Road
Memphis, Tennessee 38120 • 757-6400

Tours of the Weather Service, which is located within Agricenter International, are available. See Agricenter International listing in Chapter 1 for more information.

PIGGLY WIGGLY FOOD STORE
1620 Madison Avenue
Memphis, Tennessee 38104 • 272-0171

This great tour for even the kindergarten child includes a walk-through of the entire store, with stops in the produce section, back rooms, freezers, the meat department, and the kitchen.

Tours: Available Monday through Friday, the best time to tour is usually between 8 a.m. and 11 a.m. The tour is of interest to children 5 years old through junior high. No limit on the size of the group. Make advance reservations a day or two ahead of your desired tour time.

Admission: FREE.

PIZZA HUT
1961 Union Avenue
Memphis, Tennessee 38104 • 726-1456

Children learn firsthand the art of pizza-making when they make their own pizza in this lively tour.

Tours: Call at least a week in advance to check on availability and make reservations. Groups are limited to 30 children. Children also receive a real "Pizza Chef Certificate" upon completion of the tour.

Admission: FREE.

POLICE STATIONS

Tours: All precincts and police training sites within the city of Memphis offer tours for children of all ages. The tour includes the roll call room, equipment rooms, the police car lot, and detectives' offices. At the North Precinct you can even see an unoccupied jail! The tour lasts about 30 minutes. Call your local precinct for an appointment. (See Blue Pages in the phone Book, under **City of Memphis, Police Department.**)

Admission: FREE.

T.E. MAXSON WASTEWATER TREATMENT FACILITY
Located in the EARTH Complex at the end of Mitchell Road
Memphis, Tennessee 38109 • 789-0510

Children from fourth grade on up can see and follow each step in the process of how our city's wastewater is cleaned and recycled. Tour hour, between 7 a.m. and 3:30 p.m. Call in advance for an appointment. FREE.

TENNESSEE GINS INC.
800 Tennessee Avenue
P.O. Box 370
Covington, Tennessee 38019 • 476-2228 or 476-7842

Built in 1972 and serving a farming area with approximately a 40-mile radius, Tennessee Gins is the second largest automated cotton gin in the world. In this huge processing plant, the cotton product is "never touched by human hands." The massive machines, including hydraulic sucks, automatic strappers, lint cutters, and automated presses, do the work that once was performed manually. The very educational tour is entertaining at any time of year, but is most interesting during the fall harvesting season, when the machinery can actually be seen in operation 24 hours a day. A bonus during the growing season is the miniature cotton crop planted on the grounds for up-close viewing.

Tours: To arrange for a tour, call and ask for Mr. L.C. Thomas or Mr. Major Daniel, or simply drop in, and the pleasant staff will try to make on-the-spot arrangements. Summer hours are 8 a.m.-4:30 p.m. Monday through Friday.

Admission: FREE.

Directions: In the North Industrial Park, off Highway 51 in Covington.

UNITED STATES POST OFFICE
555 South Third Street
Memphis, Tennessee 38101 • 521-2100

Children of all ages have loved touring this facility for years. They see postal workers, mail trucks, and the inner workings of the mail system.

Tours: Although no tours are given in December or January, only a few weeks' notice is needed to make your reservation. Tour days are Monday and Tuesday at 9 a.m., 10 a.m., or 11 a.m. Tour length is one hour. Maximum group size is 25 children.

Admission: FREE.

WKNO TELEVISION AND RADIO STATION 900
900 Getwell Road
Memphis, Tennessee • 458-2521

TV's Channel 10 and FM radio station 91.1, Memphis' public broadcasting systems, offer a wonderful tour for children. Kids find out what is involved in producing a television show. Escorted right into the studio by the tour guide, they are given explanations of cameras and lights. A trip to the control room and the print and art shop demonstrates what actually goes on behind the scenes. To make the tour complete, everyone is taken to the radio booth and permitted to ask questions of the disc jockey if the program format allows.

Tours: Minimum age recommended for the tour is 5 years; maximum group size is 25 people. Scheduling ahead of time is essential since tours are not possible during some months because of major station functions. January, February, most summer months, and early fall are good prospects. The best times are mid-morning through 4 p.m. Call ahead to make an appointment.

Admission: FREE.

TRANSPORTATION:
CARS, BOATS, TRAINS, AND PLANES

The first sentence out of the mouths of many babes is something like, "Go bye-bye in car?" Children love anything that moves: they love to ride in it or point at it or imitate its sound or engage in any number of acts of admiration for the vehicle. Especially fascinating to little kids are the unusual modes of transportation — police cars, taxis, backhoes, airplanes, helicopters, ambulances, mail trucks, limousines, flat-bed cars on a train. Older kids are more apt to stare on the highway at the red BMWs, speedboats on trailers, elaborate RVs with their own personal names, and fancy motorcycles. Take advantage of your child's natural enthusiasm and have some fun traveling around. Remember that, in all of life, it's often the journey itself, not the destination, that counts in the long run.

TRAINS AND BUSES

With double-decked "showboat" buses and double-length accordion-linked buses and spiffy little "trolley" buses tooling around the streets, why not plan a day's activities around a bus trip? Schedules change, so check the MATA (Memphis Area Transit Authority) brochures located all around town (the main library keeps a well-stocked supply) to stay up-to-date on what's available. Hop on a city bus with the kids; let them pop the change in the meter box; and find a seat. For the many children who have never even been on a bus this should be a real adventure! Get off the bus at a park, art museum, or shopping mall, and have some lunch. Heading home can be a relaxing, easy-conversation time in contrast to the hassles of fighting traffic. MATA has a phone line for schedule information (274-6282), or you can call their Customer Service Center at 528-2870.

We have great hopes for our historic train station, but right now it is not a recommended place for a family outing. (See Central Station listing in this chapter under "On the Horizon.") Passengers are served exclusively by AMTRAK, with several trains scheduled throughout the week. Most leave very early in the morning or very late at night, making it impractical to plan a visit around the train's arrival at the station.

AIRPLANES

Airports are one of the most intriguing spots for a child of any age. Don't wait for someone to be coming or going before you make a trip to the airport. Whether you choose a huge metropolitan airport with jumbo jets and thousands of people or a small airport with little more than a landing strip serving commuters and private planes, plan to take a day to enjoy just looking around.

Memphis International Airport is the largest airport in the tri-state area. A day's activities await you in the airport. Ticket counters, moving sidewalks, taxis, bus shuttles, baggage popping through flap-covered openings on revolving beltways, and of course the featured attraction — big jets landing and taking off — provide thrilling sights for the whole family. Restaurants, tiny specialty shops, newsstands, fast-food bars, and video arcades make the airport a city unto its own. (See also the Tours of the Working World listing for the airport later in this chapter.)

Several smaller airports in the area provide a calmer atmosphere and afford the opportunity of a closer look at how airports work. Try one of these:

DeWitt-Spain Airport
2787 North Second
Memphis, Tennessee 38127 • 358-4063

Charles Baker Airport
3870 Fite Road
Millington, Tennessee 38053 • 873-3838

Olive Branch Airport
8000 Terminal Drive
Olive Branch, Mississippi • TN telephone # 521-9439

Arlington Airport
5793 Airline Road
Arlington, Tennessee • 867-2120

AMR-Combs (formerly Memphis Aero)
2540 Winchester
Memphis, Tennessee 38116 • 345-4700

Rows and rows of different-colored private planes and small streamlined jets of all sizes and shapes are lined up looking like they are under inspection. Ask to peek inside the hangars if the airport employees are not too busy, and have your questions ready!

Don't forget to check out **The Memphis Belle,** the B-17 bomber made famous in World War II. Located on Mud Island, it is a fascinating look at the past. Aeronautics buffs must not miss this treasure. (See the Mud Island listing in Chapter 1 for more information.)

──────── TROLLEY CARS ────────

Almost a reality now, the imported trolley cars are sure to be a big hit with Downtown shoppers and travelers. The tracks are being laid, and the ground is being prepared for the trolley station. Watch news releases for updates on the progress of our developing trolley system. (See separate listing for Trolley Cars in "On the Horizon" at the end of Chapter 2.)

MUD ISLAND MONORAIL

One track that is already laid and has been in operation for several years now is the monorail leading from the entrance on Front Street to Mud Island. Fast, quiet, and efficient, the monorail gives a sense of future travel as it glides through the air over the river far below. The ride itself is worth a visit to Mud Island. Operates seasonally.

DELTA DUCKS

Actually World War II vintage military amphibious craft, the Delta Ducks are a genuine treat for young and old. The ducks' land and water sightseeing tour takes passengers through downtown Memphis, then splashes into the Wolf River and cruises along to various points of interest along the shoreline. The tour lasts about an hour and a half. Tours begins at Delta Duckport, 125 N. Front Street, Memphis, Tennessee 38103 (576-6385).

HORSE-DRAWN CARRIAGE RIDES

To get a real feel for downtown Memphis at a leisurely pace, try one of the many carriage companies. Included in the 30-minute ride is a tour of Main Street, a look at Historic Beale Street, and views of parks and the Hernando de Soto Bridge. The cost runs about $25 for two people, with a charge of $8 for each additional person. Pick up a carriage at the Union Avenue entrance of The Peabody or at the corner of Beale Street and Third. If you wish to call ahead and reserve a carriage, companies are listed in the _Yellow Pages_ under **Carriage — Hire**.

CARS

For families that include car enthusiasts, there are several annual car shows held in Memphis. Usually held at the **Memphis Cook Convention Center**, 255 N. Main (576-1200), where every inch is marked by a shiny auto, these shows are sometimes a trip into the future and then again a trip into the past. The **Mid-South Sports Show,** held in March, is something to watch for. This show features all kinds of cars, boats, RVs, trailers, and just about anything else that moves. Kids love climbing through the "home-like" RVs or sitting behind the steering wheel of a futuristic car. **Antique Autos** also have their show time during the year. You can call the convention center to find out what's coming up.

During the **Mid-South Fair,** held at the Mid-South Fairgrounds the last two weeks in September, an entire building is dedicated to new cars, trucks, jeeps, and mini vans. While enjoying the fair, be sure to check out the transportation building. The *Playbook* section of *The Commercial Appeal* will also list upcoming automobile shows.

BOATS

One of the first places you are sure to visit in Memphis will also be one of the best places to see the widest variety of boats around. Any time of year, in any kind of weather, take a trip down to the banks of the Mississippi River. Paddlewheel boats, tugboats, Coast Guard fireboats, glamorous yachts, majestic sailboats, and family pleasure boats are out and about on the river. Rows and rows of boats of all kinds can be seen docked on the banks of Mud Island. (See the listing in Chapter 2 for the Memphis Queen Line for information about a special boat tour, and check Chapter 5 for information about canoe rentals and raft trips.)

There is also the **Memphis Boat Show,** held each January at the Memphis Cook Convention Center, 255 N. Main (576-1200). Every boating accessory you've ever been curious about will be on display. Boating exhibitors from all over the Mid-South are ready to answer questions and let the kids pretend they're out on the lake. Don't forget to check *The Commercial Appeal* listings for additional shows coming to the area.

AND MORE . . .

While on the subject of transportation, be sure to visit your local fire station, post office, police station, or neighborhood construction sites to see a variety of work vehicles.

PETS AND ANIMALS

Even if your family includes a shaggy dog, two spotted cats, a nocturnal gerbil, and a tank of fancy fish, your kids probably think they need another pet! Children are drawn to animals as if to a magnet. Witness the crowds at the Memphis Zoo and Aquarium. Children love the petting area where they can feed llamas and goats and watch the kangaroos hop. Feeling an animal's wet tongue brings squeals of delight, and touching the coarse fur brings faces of wonder. There are additional spots around town that can be great fun for families that love animals. Observing, learning, and getting acquainted with the unusual are a part of any adventure. This is one we think you'll "go ape over."

ANIMAL SHELTERS AND HUMANE SOCIETIES

The diverse animals at the animal shelters in the area are always eager to greet visitors. Before your visit, talk to your child about whether this is just a "looking" trip or there is a real possibility that you're shopping for a new "family member." Without this discussion on the front end, you may have a sadly disappointed companion on the way home. You might also discuss in advance the conditions to expect at the shelter, where many pets must share a relatively small space. If your child is extremely sensitive, a visit to an animal shelter may be almost too heartbreaking to bear.

Animals that are lost or abandoned, but otherwise healthy, find their way to the **Memphis Animal Shelter** or other area shelters. A self-guided tour of the maze of cages makes it hard to leave without a pet. The animals are divided by size, and you'll probably see more breeds than you knew were possible. All these pets are in need of good homes and are ready to cuddle up to their new families.

The **Memphis Humane Society** helps sick or injured animals virtually all over the city and most of Shelby County. Although some of the rehabilitated pets are available for adoption, this is not the major focus of the Humane Society. Adoption-eligible animals are dewormed, bathed, partially inoculated against disease, and spayed or neutered, then pictured in the Society's newsletter, *Paw Prints*. The staff is ready and willing to make presentations to groups of children from preschool through high school. A special club named PAWS for kids ages 10-18 has been formed. This is a junior auxiliary group of young volunteers dedicated to improving animal welfare. Insurance liabilities preclude direct contact with the animals, but PAWS members enjoy knowing that they are definitely helping animals. Meetings are held once a month at the main library on Peabody. The Humane Society also holds a marvelous annual Christmas bazaar, with lunch, crafts, and photo opportunities with Santa for your pet. Other fund-raising events and contests are held throughout the year.

Call the numbers below for more information about visiting hours and pet adoption:

Bartlett Humane Society
5730 Ferguson
Bartlett, Tennessee 38134 • 387-0753

Germantown Animal Shelter
7700 Southern
Germantown, Tennessee 38138 • 757-7358

Memphis Animal Shelter
3456 Tchulahoma Road
Memphis, Tennessee 38118 • 362-5310

Memphis Humane Society
2238 Central Avenue
Memphis, Tennessee 38104 • 272-1753

PET STORES

Unless you have a heart of stone, you probably always give in to your child's tug and plea to enter every pet store you pass at every shopping mall. All these stores have a variety of cute, furry dogs; shiny, sleek cats; brightly colored birds; and fish of all sizes and shapes. The stores are fun to visit and have all the new-fangled gadgets that go along with pet ownership. We have found some pet stores that require a bit more effort than stepping a few feet off the mall aisle, but they are well worth the extra effort. Just ask the little one jumping up and down beside you.

Ruby Begonia's Pet Emporium is located at 234 Cooper Avenue in Midtown (276-6047). If you hear noisy chatter here, don't be surprised to find that the talking is coming from some source other than human. Myna birds and parrots, parakeets and finches are perched throughout the store. Rows of fish tanks rival any aquarium. And there's more! Cuddly rabbits, gerbils, hamsters, guinea pigs, and mice are well represented, along with snakes, lizards, and spiders. The helpful crew on duty is full of information, but remember here (and at any other pet store) that this is a store, not a petting zoo. Try not to handle unless you are serious about a purchase.

For even more exotic birds, fish, and reptiles, try **Amazon Pets**, 4326 State Road, Memphis (382-5916).

Not a pet store at all, **Goodwin's Greenhouses** at 2238 Sunset Road in Germantown (754-7293) probably ought to be. It has one of the most fascinating collections of animals you'll find anywhere around town. From caged tarantulas, rabbits, and parrots to wandering pigs, dogs, cats, and roosters, the animals seem perfectly at home in their "tropical" surroundings. This is one greenhouse where the parents can shop for rhododendron and spider fern to their hearts' content while the kids are royally amused by the roving creatures.

For a treat unequaled for the well-established pet owner or the aspiring pet owner, we have found a real treasure. **Hot Dogs & Cool Cats**, 926 S. Cooper, Memphis (272-1200), is a self-service pet-washing, pet-photography studio and pet emporium featuring unusual gifts for the most discriminating pet. Open 11 a.m. to 7 p.m. seven days a week, it is unlike anything we have seen anywhere else . . . yet.

PET SHOWS

An urge to see the "best of the best" is the reason for all kinds of shows, and pet owners are just as eager as anyone else to show off their sweeties' exemplary characteristics. Kids love to watch animals perform and to compare different breeds and variations within a breed at pet shows. Most **purebreed championship shows** are held at the Mid-South Fairgrounds. Sponsored by the Memphis Kennel Club (867-2357) or by individual purebreed clubs (i.e., Doberman Pinscher Club, Siamese Cat Club, etc.), shows are held periodically; the times are usually announced in *The Commercial Appeal.* There is usually an **all-breed championship** held twice a year (fall and spring). A popular all-breed cat show, **M.I.C.E.**, is an annual show held in November.

On the lighter side, amateur pet shows and parades are routinely held at parks and recreation centers. Watch for listings in neighborhood newsletters, newspapers, and television news shows.

ANIMAL FARMS

Happy Times Farm, nestled just outside Memphis in the lush surroundings of farmland and forests at 4965 Reynolds Road, Collierville, Tennessee, is more than just an animal farm. Although self-described as a petting zoo, Happy Times is much, much more. On group trips out to the farm, kids are invited not only to feed the chickens, donkeys, and lambs, but also to churn butter, take a pony for a spin, or ride a miniature train around the property. While taking a walking tour of the farm, kids might see a pumpkin patch or a small lake complete with ducks. Happy Times Farm has more delights to offer than you are likely to imagine. Handlers and owners will also bring pony cart rides, "sleigh rides," and farm animals to YOU. For a special group gathering or birthday party, call Happy Times Farm at 853-9642 to get information on the programs offered there.

SMALL ART MUSEUMS, GALLERIES, AND ART CENTERS

Parents who dare to venture into art museums with youngsters in tow are often surprised at the positive reaction from children who are allowed to explore at their own pace without too much lecturing to make the outing a "worthwhile experience." The same can be said for many smaller art collections found at commercial galleries. Children may not feel so overwhelmed in the smaller surroundings, and parents may not feel the pressure to see everything in a gallery without an admission charge. Art galleries can present an especially appealing opportunity on a cold or rainy day for a family experience.

We have selected a variety of small galleries, from the fairly traditional to the rather avant-garde. We believe that there is something here to interest everyone. If your family finds a particularly appealing gallery, you might ask about similar ones around town. Artists, we have found, are for the most part a community-oriented, helpful lot.

Most of the galleries listed have openings about once a month, often festive affairs. The best place to keep track of what's showing is in local news listings. The Friday *Playbook* section and the Sunday *Fanfare* section of *The Commercial Appeal* are two excellent places to look. *Memphis* magazine, *The Memphis Flyer*, and other local regular publications are other good places to check. Most galleries are happy to add potential customers to their mailing lists for notification of openings.

Some of the galleries below have special open houses during the holidays or joint openings in the summer (i.e., Memphis Art Gallery Association's July show).

We have tried to provide a guide to hours of operation for each gallery, but many galleries are short-staffed. They are happy to arrange for openings by appointment to compensate for brief regular hours of business, though.

ALBERS FINE ART GALLERY
1102 Brookfield Road
Memphis, Tennessee 38119 • 683-2256

Defining itself as "a commercial gallery with the attitude of a small museum," Albers features respected contemporary regional and national artists. The exhibits usually change monthly, offering families a variety of visual stimulation in bold designs and innovative techniques. The art on display is not the only treat awaiting visitors at Albers. The gallery space itself earned an architectural award for its museum-quality design. Highlights include changes in color and pattern of hardwood floors and a teardrop shape formed in the ceiling above. This gallery could be an excellent place to introduce a child to the world of art in a space small enough to please without overwhelming.

Hours: Tuesday-Friday 9:30 a.m.-5 p.m.; Saturday, 11 a.m.-3 p.m.

ART VILLAGE GALLERY
333 Beale Street
Memphis, Tennessee 38103 • 521-0782

Art Village Gallery features African, Caribbean, and South American artists, many of whose works are of great interest to families and children. A past presentation included a display of what life is like in a traditional African village; children as well as adults found it to be very exciting. Shows change every two months, and every February the gallery presents a special exhibit in honor of Black History Month.

Hours: Tuesday-Thursday, 12:30-5:30 p.m.; Friday-Saturday, 12:30-8 p.m.

Admission: FREE.

ARTIFACTS GALLERY
1007 Oakhaven
Memphis, Tennessee 38119 • 767-5236

Artifacts Gallery, which names as its goal "the discovery, wonder, and exuberance of fine craft art," offers works in wood, clay, metal, fiber, and other media by regional and national American craft artists. Past exhibits of particular interest to children include the life-like soft-sculpture animals and the carved wooden boxes with hidden "architectural," swing-out compartments. A recent show displayed mobiles of different sizes, shapes, and colors. The acquisitions focus here seems to be on whimsy, which is sure to enchant children.

Hours: Tuesday-Saturday, noon-6 p.m.

BELL-ROSS GALLERY
1080 Brookfield Road
Memphis, Tennessee 38119 • 682-2189

Contemporary, impressionist, and folk painting; glass, marble, and bronze sculpture; and elegant, one-of-a-kind gold and silver jewelry give a hint of the variety offered in the exhibitions at Bell-Ross Gallery. The regional and national artists selected for shows at Bell-Ross present works that are imaginative and brightly attractive, even to children who think they don't like art galleries. No child could resist, for example, the surrealistic images of local artist Annabelle Meachem, who describes her ideas as deriving from her dreams.

Hours: Tuesday-Saturday, 9 a.m.-5 p.m.

BINGHAM-KURTS GALLERY
766 S. White Station Road
Memphis, Tennessee 38119 • 683-6200

For contemporary paintings and sculpture from renowned regional artists, Bingham-Kurts Gallery is a must. Exhibits change monthly, with the Christmas exhibit being of particular interest to children. A past Christmas theme, "Folk, Fantasy, and Function," intrigued children with fantastic animals and whimsical art. Located in a condominium complex with architecture of French influence, Bingham-Kurts Gallery has an additional location in downtown Memphis open by appointment only (527-2787).

Hours: White Station location: Tuesday-Friday, 10 a.m.-5:30 p.m.;
Saturday, 11 a.m.-4 p.m.

CLOUGH HANSON GALLERY
Rhodes College
2000 North Parkway
Memphis, Tennessee 38112 • 726-3000

This small, tasteful gallery on Rhodes College campus features a variety of artwork. Weavings, pottery, watercolor, and sculpture (but not all at once!) are just a few of the exhibits you might expect to see on a given visit. Some shows will appeal more to children than others.

Hours: Monday-Friday, 9 a.m.-5.p.m. Call to find out what's on
exhibit.

COOPER STREET GALLERY
964 S. Cooper
Memphis, Tennessee 38104 • 272-7053

For the actual smell of paint and feel of a working studio, this gallery is tops. Presenting primarily "noncommercially viable art by young (or young-ish) artists," the gallery provides an outlet of expression for very contemporary, alternative art. Children's artwork is featured regularly in such shows as the annual exhibition of collaborations between established artists and their own children. Be ready, when entering Cooper Street Gallery, to view such radical scenes as the rear of a papier mache pick-up truck projecting from the wall (complete with papier mache dogs) or an oil painting of a contented pig lounging on an elegant sofa. A gift table offers for sale such items as T-shirts, oil-painted masonite magnets, and small original oil paintings.

Hours: Wednesday, Friday, and Saturday, 11 a.m.-5 p.m.; other times by appointment.

Admission: FREE, but donations are gratefully accepted in a glass bowl at the entrance.

EADS GALLERIES AND GROUNDS
12382 Washington Road
Eads, Tennessee 38028 • 867-8100

This "log cabin community" in rural Eads, Tennessee, a suburb of Memphis, gives new meaning to the word "unusual." Every foot of the free-spirited grounds (or "gardens," as director Jimmy Crosthwait likes to refer to them) and of the cluster of quaintly individualized freestanding galleries throbs with the essence of Crosthwait — sculptor, puppeteer, purveyor of excellence. Belying a youthful three years of existence, the art center seems closer in spirit to the '60s than the '90s. The unconventional Crosthwait himself, with long locks and grizzled beard, embodies the older, wiser, peace-loving flower child of the '60s. His personalized tour of the galleries and grounds is philosophical and instructive and unlike the gallery tour one is apt to encounter anywhere else.

The galleries include Gallery #1, recently showing "ice box art" (or artist-created, one-of-a-kind magnets) mounted on, naturally, old refrigerator doors; the Photography Gallery, where the work of about 10 photographers is rotated every six weeks to two months; the Gift Shop, featuring affordably priced local and regional crafts items; and the Ceramics Studio, which is housed in Eads' old post office (the new post office is a stone's throw down the road). The grounds are dominated by two old gas pumps with stained glass windows that are lit up at night and by Crosthwait's sculpture — his Perseus fountain made of welded steel and rocks, his ornamental iron archway, his "Eads Beads" arch, and outcroppings of his "Zen chimes" (unlike wind chimes in that they produce "the sound of only one hand clapping").

Seasonal events of particular interest to families include the annual crafts fair (held in the spring or the fall) and the annual bonfire (held just before Thanksgiving), which was coupled in 1991 with a sheepherding and sharpshooting affair. A statewide sculpture competition slated for the spring of 1992 will be kicked off with a nine-hole miniature golf competition (each hole designed by a different sculptor).

If you forget to bring along a picnic to Eads Galleries, you are likely to be directed to Vinegar Jim's, a wonderful restaurant resembling an authentic 1890s tavern and featuring good, substantial down-home food at very reasonable prices. It is definitely worth the 15-minute drive.

Hours: Eads Galleries must close from the beginning of January through most of April, when it is "held hostage by the elements." The rest of the year it is open from 1-6 p.m. on Saturdays and Sundays or by appointment.

Directions: From Memphis, take I-40 toward Nashville. Take Exit #18 (Highway 64) east. Drive seven miles to the Collierville-Arlington Road (Rt. 205). Turn right (south); then go half a mile and turn left on Washington.

EATON GALLERY
968 June Road
Memphis, Tennessee 38119 • 767-0690

Eaton Gallery is unique among the smaller galleries in the area as it exhibits not only contemporary art, but also more traditional art, including portrait work. Local, regional, and national artists are represented in the gallery. Every year during Memphis in May, Eaton Gallery hosts an exhibition of art from the country being honored. In 1990, when the honored country was France, Eaton Gallery was presented an award for an outstanding community event.

Hours: Tuesday-Friday, 11 a.m.-5 p.m.; Saturday, noon-4 p.m. or by appointment.

GALLERY THREE FIVE O
350 S. Main
Memphis, Tennessee 38103 • 526-6583

Located in the South Main Historic District of downtown Memphis, Gallery Three Five O is only a few blocks from the National Civil Rights Museum. (It will also be on the trolley line that is currently under construction.) The commercial gallery features clothing, paintings, games, books, jewelry, and other pieces of art and artifacts by local and national African-American artists.

Hours: Monday-Saturday, 11 a.m.-6 p.m.; Sunday, 4-7 p.m.

MARBLE SHOWROOM
1557 Madison Avenue
Memphis, Tennessee 38104 • 272-9505

Marble Showroom is a full-service gallery, featuring multimedia exhibits. The building that houses the showroom — an old bakery — is a treat in itself. What was once the Tastee-Bread Bakery is now home of the Memphis Design Center. The atrium in the center of the building is a focal point for the gallery. Also located within the Center is **Madison Gallery**. Both galleries are relatively new on the art scene and plan to offer shows of special interest to families and children. Exhibits change every six to eight weeks.

Hours: Monday-Saturday, 10 a.m.-6 p.m.

MEMPHIS COLLEGE OF ART
Overton Park
Memphis, Tennessee 38112 • 726-4085

Memphis College of Art, situated in beautiful Overton Park, is the Mid-South's only professional art college. Established in 1936 (previously named Memphis Academy of Arts), the college moved in 1959 to its present building in Overton Park. The institution confers both under-graduate and graduate degrees, and it extends its programs to the community through continuing and professional education classes, the Saturday school and advanced placement classes.

Never sure of what will be waiting in the three galleries, which rotate exhibits, a visitor here might find work by students, faculty, or guest artists. Etched glass, handmade paper, woven textiles, computer-gener-ated graphic designs, oil paintings on canvas, line drawings, and clay sculpture are just a few of the many diverse media that might be found on a given visit. Children especially enjoy the annual April show featuring the works of the Saturday school scholars (ages 2 1/2-18).

Regardless of what's on exhibit, a trip to the College of Art galleries is sure to offer a pleasant respite in a busy day, a place to view some interesting art without the pressure having to "see it all" in a large museum.

Programs of particular interest to families include the Saturday school and the summer programs for children ages 2 1/2-18, the advanced placement classes for high school juniors and seniors (participants chosen in September from previously submitted portfolios), the continu-ing and professional education program for adults (fall, spring, and summer programs), and the popular December holiday bazaar, when student artwork may be purchased.

A snack bar and supply store, both open to the public, are in operation from 9 a.m. till 2 p.m. Monday through Friday. Rest rooms and water fountains available. Free parking is available on the street. There is full accessibility to the handicapped.

Hours: Monday-Friday, 8:30 a.m.-4:30 p.m.; Saturday, 10 a.m.-noon.

Admission: FREE.

Directions: From Poplar Avenue, enter Overton Park at Kenilworth Place, and veer to the left at the Y.

MEMPHIS STATE UNIVERSITY GALLERY
3750 Norriswood
Communication and Fine Arts Building
Memphis State University
Memphis, Tennessee 38152 • 678-2224

A component of the Memphis State University Department of Art, the 10-year-old University Gallery houses the well-known and much-respected Institute of Egyptian Art and Archaeology (call 678-2555 for more information about the Institute). Hosting three student shows per year, the University Gallery also features changing exhibits with a focus on nationally recognized contemporary artists.

The major permanent exhibits — the Neil Nokes collection of West African masks, the antiquities from 3,500 years of Egyptian history (including sculpture, a mummy, papyruses, and implements), and the Gruenberg collection of miniature interiors (the appropriate contents of a dollhouse encased in wall displays) — enthrall children and their parents alike.

School groups frequently enjoy sketching in the gallery (pencils only); and excellent educator's guides for the Egyptian and African collections are available to teachers. Free activity sheets are offered to all children in the Egyptian Antiquities gallery. Docent-guided tours are available to groups with previous arrangements.

On-campus metered parking spaces are available. Stop by the Visitor Information Center at Central and Patterson for instructions. Sufficient advance notice to the University Gallery might allow the staff time to send you a card for waived parking fees. Handicapped accessible.

Hours: Tuesday-Friday, 9 a.m.-5 p.m.; Saturday-Sunday, 1-5 p.m. (Closed on Mondays and during exhibition changes.)

Admission: FREE.

RICHARDS GALLERY
2281 Central Avenue
Memphis, Tennessee 38104 • 278-0490

Tucked away on a tiny hill in midtown Memphis, this small gallery is a delightful stop for a family looking for something different. The Richards Gallery is family-owned. It features southwestern and contemporary art, along with an outrageous collection of exquisite minerals from all over the world.

The collection of art centers around artists from Arizona, New Mexico, California, and Nevada, but also has regional art represented. Hand-beaded moccasins, silver jewelry and terra cotta sculptures are packed into this well-detailed gallery. Ah, but the minerals . . . Quartz and alabaster, along with strange and exotic variations from far-off lands, are shined to perfection. Kids will have a hard time pulling themselves away from the displays.

Hours: Monday-Saturday, 10 a.m.-5 p.m.

SHAINBERG GALLERY
Jewish Community Center
6560 Poplar Avenue
Memphis, Tennessee 38138 • 761-0810

Although most of the activities held at the Jewish Community Center are for members only, the Shainberg Gallery is a fine arts gallery open to everyone. The small, one-room gallery is packed with paintings, jewelry, crafts, and sculpture. The exhibit changes almost once a month and is designed to be appropriate for families. The gallery is located to the left

147

as you enter the community center's main entrance. (Jewish Community Center also offers live theatre presentations at its Centerstage. The season schedule is open to the public.)

Hours: Monday-Thursday, 9 a.m.-5 p.m.; Friday, 9 a.m.-4 p.m.; Sunday, 10 a.m.-6 p.m.

VANCE GALLERY
4646 Poplar Avenue
Memphis, Tennessee 38117 • 767-7940

Vance Gallery exhibits mostly traditional and impressionist works of national and European artists. Although primarily oriented toward adults, the gallery will occasionally display art which might be of interest to children. Call ahead to find out what's on exhibit.

Hours: Monday-Saturday, 10:30 a.m.-4:30 p.m.

WORKING SPACE GALLERY
2541 Broad Avenue
Memphis, Tennessee 38112 • 327-9005

Almost hidden on a block of used appliance stores, print shops, and small specialty bargain centers, the Working Space Gallery offers modern multi-media exhibits, many of which might be of interest to youngsters. With stark white walls and contemporary touches, this intimate gallery is situated in an area of town striving for revitalization. Other galleries are suddenly appearing in the neighborhood, with showings by appointment only. Call ahead to find out what is on display.

Hours: Friday-Saturday, 10 a.m.-6 p.m.

SHOPPING AND HOBBIES

Just about everyone enjoys shopping of one type or another. Whether your family enjoys toy try-outs, clothes modeling, hardware experimenta tion, or mall browsing, there is surely something to hold your interest in Memphis. And there are places to find the accoutrements for just about any hobby or skill — from magic tricks to model trains to tea party etiquette.

TOY STORES

If you can ride it, or rattle it, or crawl in it, or jump on it, or read it, or rock it, or bounce it, you can probably find it at one of these large chain toy stores: **Children's Palace** (4835 American Way and 3481 Austin Peay); **Circus World** (Southland Mall, Oak Court Mall, and Raleigh Springs Mall); **Kay Bee Toys** (Hickory Ridge Mall and Mall of Memphis); and **Toys "R" Us** (South Perkins Road next to Mall of Memphis). All of these giant stores offer just about any kind of toy or game that a kid of just about any age could have a yen for.

If you're looking for something a little bit different and you want a smaller setting than the toy giants, you might try one of the quaint little shops listed below. Your selection will be more limited, but what you find will be unusual and delightful to any child on your gift list.

Choo-Choo Children's Books and Toys
4615-14 Poplar Avenue • 761-5366

Fantastic costumes, learning toys, books, storytelling and performance sessions, and a play area for small children make Choo-Choo's special.

Embraceable Zoo
Hickory Ridge Mall • 367-2488

This "zoo" is filled with a huge variety of stuffed animals — from monkeys to elephants. Go in and hug to your heart's content.

Hearts and Pines
3092 Poplar Avenue in Chickasaw Oaks Mall • 458-1939

Beautiful collectors' dolls, toys from all over the world, and hands-on learning toys are some of the treats here.

Miniature Gallery
3554 Park Avenue
Memphis • 398-6464

It's fun for children OR adults to look at the fantastic selection of dollhouses and accessories and then pretend . . .

Only Kids
6150 Poplar Avenue • 683-1234

"All a kids' store should be . . ." is the goal of Only Kids. You'll find toys of all kinds, including handmade ones from all around the world, clothing, shoes, books, and a HAIR SALON just for kids. Storytelling and performance sessions available on weekends.

Village Toymaker
7850 Poplar Avenue, Suite 12
Germantown • 755-3309

This toy shop features fine dolls, dollhouses, dollhouse furniture, and toys from around the world.

HOBBIES

How many children do you know who collect rocks . . . pine cones . . . stamps . . . coins . . . dolls . . . or WHATEVER? Children are natural collectors, seeing everything as precious and unique. Collecting joins model building, arts and crafts, reading, photography, and computers as one of the favorite hobby-time activities of children. Their hobbies become their parents' hobbies, and everyone ends up learning about the subject. There are several hobby shops listed in the Yellow Pages under **Hobby & Model Shops**. These shops are up-to-date on any **Collectors Fairs** coming to the area. Bookstores usually have a section devoted to topics dealing with hobbies and collections. Don't be afraid to expand your horizons. Even if model railroading isn't among your family's hobbies, you might want to visit the **Model Railroad and Hobby Shop** (3436 Park Avenue, Memphis, 324-7245), which has a great display of all kinds of trains and their accessories. Whether you're an amateur magician or not, you shouldn't miss **The Fun Shop** at 634 S. Highland (324-3274).

The weekend Flea Market at the Mid-South Fairgrounds is an additional source for the avid collector. Anything old, peculiar, bizarre, or irregular seems to find its way to one of the many tables. If your child doesn't already have a hobby, a trip to the flea market will surely spark an interest. The _Playbook_ section of the Friday _Commercial Appeal_ lists all kinds of fairs. Whether the events feature antiques, dolls, toys, baseball cards, comics, gems and minerals, or ships in bottles, you'll want to "collect" the members of your family, pile in the car, and check them out.

Here is a hobby for your child that might make your grocery shopping trips a bit easier: **Piggly Wiggly Pals Club.** Kids ages 4 to 10 have a special invitation from all local Piggly Wiggly grocery stores. The Piggly Wiggly Pals Club began accepting applications for membership in September, 1991. The children who register receive free stickers, iron-on transfers, and other prizes just for visiting the store with their parents. Look for the red and yellow stars hanging over the Pals Club Corner in any local Piggly Wiggly for more information.

If your daughter is interested in tea parties and the proper etiquette to accompany, you might check out **Goldsmith's White Gloves and Party Manners.** Goldsmith's, Memphis' best-known department store, offers regularly a six-week course entitled "White Gloves and Party Manners" for the benefit of "young ladies ages 5 to 10." With the expected reward of courtesy and refinement for their daughters, parents gladly pay the $60 course fee. Call 766-4145 for more information.

If your child is still searching for a hobby after all this exploration, you might head over to the main library on Peabody Avenue. Listed in the "Club Book" there, you'll find numerous special-interest clubs available in the Memphis area that capitalize on a child's interest in birds, cameras, coins, dolls, trains, home computers, postcards, and even the _Star Trek_ series. Happy hobbies!

HARDWARE STORES

A universal adventure for youngsters is a Saturday morning trip to the hardware store. Parents are often surprised by their children's delight in this outing and then doubly surprised at the unusual items the kids unearth in their explorations around the store. Hardware stores are usually teeming with not just the expected nuts and bolts, hammers and door locks, but also with such oddities as food mills, double boilers, rat traps in graduated sizes, drawer knobs, and oodles of other enticing bins of "neat junk." Here are a few places to try with your child. **Stewart Brothers Hardware Company**, 1340 Madison Avenue (726-1922), has everything from cast-iron cornbread pans to brass doorknobs. An assortment of treasures, some dating back, others new-fangled gadgets can be found. **C.E. Thompson Builderway**, 2600 Southern Avenue (324-4425), becomes a roaming adventure of peeking in cabinets, looking at machinery, and helping count nails. One of the most unusual lumber stores around is **Colco Fine Woods and Tools**, 2631 Jackson Avenue (452-9663). Wood from all over the world can be touched, smelled, and compared. **Gate City Hardware and Paint Company**, 2500 Summer Avenue (458-3050), has about two or three stores' worth of odds and ends packed into its small quarters. We've provided a sample of intriguing hardware stores; get your child to help you find your own favorite.

SCHOOL SUPPLY/OFFICE SUPPLY STORES

Even though kids tire of the school-year routine and all the tools that go with their trade, they never seem to tire of the places that stockpile paper, pencils, erasers, staplers, and the other "hardware" of school life. Office supply stores can entertain children who like to "play school" or "play office" for hours. You should be able to locate one near you by looking in the Yellow Pages under **Office Supplies**. Even more fascinating for children are stores that sell not only basic paper goods, but also workbooks, stickers, gradebooks, and other tools of the teacher's trade. **Al Graci**, 1217 Getwell Road (324-9251), and **American School and Office Products**, 3964 Jackson Avenue (382-0700), are two of the biggest and best. Others can be found in the *Yellow Pages* under **School Supplies**.

MALLS WITH A FLAIR

The strip shopping centers of the '50s have given way to the all-weather shopping malls we take for granted today. Shoppers leave their cars in the parking lot and spend a whole day shopping, eating, and being entertained in the mall collection of shops, including all the amenities of a small town. Some of the most interesting malls in Memphis are listed here.

Hickory Ridge Mall
Winchester Road at Ridgeway

Packed with upscale clothing shops, a food court, a movie theatre, bookstores, and all the other requisites of a top-notch suburban shopping mall, Hickory Ridge offers the bonus of attractive design featuring interesting sculptures around a sunken stage area and the *piece de resistance*, a contemporary, double-decker Italian carousel, where shoppers may ride a carved pony or spinning cup for 50 cents.

Mall of Memphis
American Way at Perkins Extended

Newly remodeled with an art deco design, Mall of Memphis is more attractive than in the past, but what truly distinguishes it from other shopping centers is the ice rink in the center of the first floor. Diners at the second-floor food court enjoy watching classes, competitive events, or just casual skaters on the ice below.

Oak Court Mall
Poplar Avenue and Perkins Extended

Known by some small children as the "ball mall," this is the one in midtown Memphis with the giant marble ball constantly revolving on its watery stand. The decor includes a well-appointed open theatre area with big windows looking out on a green area and a number of interesting body-in-motion sculptures. The stores are the basic ones you'd expect in a solid shopping mall. But don't come looking for a movie theatre here: you'll be disappointed.

AND OTHERS . . .

Some shopping spots are just simply wonderful — not because they offer practical items for sale or because they are beautifully designed or because their prices are the best in town. They are wonderful because they are unique. They have a character and style all their own. They're not afraid of being different or old-fashioned or a little bizarre. We are tipping you off to some of our favorite hidden little jewels. We hope you find them enchanting enough to send you on a scavenger hunt for your own favorite secret little shopping spots to let your very best friends in on.

Champion's Pharmacy
2220 S. Third at Mallory • 946-2818

Exploring Champion's Pharmacy can be a real adventure. Offering an assortment of exotic products from goose grease to snake oil liniment, it is a place to amuse the fancy. A full-line drugstore, it sells souvenirs and displays "antiques and artifacts."

Christmas Tree Factory Outlet
2300 Kentucky Street
(Mallory exit off I-55 to Kentucky St.) • 942-4660

The cavernous warehouse that houses the Christmas Tree Factory Outlet fills each fall with rows and rows of artificial spruce, pine, fir, and other evergreens. It gives the impression of a little synthetic forest with a floor of concrete. Trees and trimmings may be purchased during the Christmas tree season from 10 a.m. to 5 p.m. Wednesdays-Sundays.

Goodwin's Greenhouses
2238 Sunset Road
Germantown • 754-7293

A combination greenhouse/laid-back zoo, Goodwin's has some of the most beautiful plants we've seen anywhere in addition to the oddest assortment of domesticated animals you're likely to find anywhere.

HOTEL HOPPING

With tourism an important part of the Memphis economy, we of course have our share of splendid accommodations ranging from the lavishly restored "Grand Old Hotels of the South" to the modern luxurious hotels of today. Without spending a penny, the family can enjoy a wide variety of elegant and magnificent establishments throughout the city. Noteworthy stops along your "hop" should start with some of our downtown favorites: **The Radisson**, with its plush lobby; **The Peabody**, with its old southern charm, ornate lobby, and, of course, The Peabody Ducks; and **The Crowne Plaza**, with its glass elevator descending directly into the lobby. Midtown Memphis finds the Cajun flair at **The French Quarter Inn**. A final stop must be made in East Memphis at the **Omni**. This hotel not only has a marvelous elevator rising on the outside of the circular mirrored building, but it even has its own small pond with ducks to feed. Of course there are many other fine hotels sprinkled across Memphis. You may get hooked on finding your favorite.

HOTEL HOP!

Even if you live in the city or are in town just for the day, visiting hotels can be a treat for all. The hustle and bustle of the travelers, conventioneers, or families being reunited can bring out your own family's conversations on a wide range of topics. Marvel at the variety of architecture you see. From the grandiose styles of the ornately renovated older hotels to the shiny, mirrored exteriors of the modern hotels, opinions and personal tastes can be compared. Tastefully decorated lobbies are the setting for great photo opportunities. On rainy days when cabin fever starts to get everyone down, an excursion to a favorite spot can be just what the gang needs to add a bit of energy to the day.

SUNDAY BRUNCH

For those families who enjoy elegant dining, several of the hotels have marvelous gourmet Sunday brunches. Lists and advertisements of these brunches appear in the Friday _Playbook_ section of _The Commercial Appeal_. Special activities for the kids during holiday seasons are often featured. Easter egg hunts complete with an Easter Bunny are often part of the festivities. Superb ice sculptures often adorn the buffet tables. Prices vary, but an average price for the brunch is $15.95 for adults and $7.95 for children (children's ages are designated differently at each location). Serving hours are usually between 10 a.m. and 2 p.m. Call for more specific information. Although some hotel restaurants do not take reservations, others require them.

ON THE HORIZON

There is always something exciting in the works in Memphis, Tennessee. That's what makes this a dynamic place to live or visit. Since anticipation is a special form of pleasure in itself, Memphians have a lot of fun waiting for the landscape to change, the opportunities to expand. By the time this book reaches your hands, the entries below will probably be realities and you'll be eagerly awaiting something else just over the rainbow, on the horizon.

CENTRAL STATION

Dilapidated Central Station, which once served as a bustling transportation hub befitting its architectural grandeur, may once again become a center of transit activity. Buses, trains, trolley cars, and other vehicles may converge on the station if it is refurbished according to a plan being promoted by Memphis Area Transit Authority.

NATIONAL FOOTBALL LEAGUE

For years local business and government leaders have vied to gain an NFL franchise for Memphis. Exhibition games have consistently drawn capacity crowds to Liberty Bowl Stadium. The current pitch is citywide in scope and support. 1992 could be the year for Memphis to land a professional football team. Keep your fingers crossed!

TOWBOAT FERRY

A Corps of Engineers towboat that used to push barges on the Mississippi River is set for retirement in 1993. A suggestion to turn the vessel into a floating hotel and excursion boat has been put before the Mississippi River Commission. Under the proposal, tourists would be ferried the 17.6 miles between Meeman-Shelby State Park and downtown Memphis. City and county government officials have not responded, but it sounds like an idea with a lot of potential.

TROLLEY

With construction well under way, the picturesque trolley system is sure to be a welcome addition to the Downtown transportation scene. The 2.5-mile route has been cleared, and tracks are being laid. The imported trolley cars have been ordered and will serve as a cheerful conveyance for passengers traveling within the hotel district and historic districts of downtown Memphis. The trolleys' main stop will feature a clock tower enhanced by music and synchronized water jets.

4. Performing Arts for Children
(Music, Dance, Theatre and Puppetry)

T he smell of sawdust . . . The taste of cotton candy . . . Discordant musical tones building toward smooth harmony . . . Ruffles, lace, and flounces on costumes evocative of another time and place . . . The fluid movement of a dancer's body . . . The conductor's baton lifted expectantly in air . . . The hush as the lights go down . . .

Whether in the form of a bawdy, smelly circus three-ring show or a white tie and tails opera affair, or anywhere in between, a live performance is electrifying in its immediacy, vibrancy, and daring.

Children are spontaneous creatures. They love variety and experimentation — as participants or spectators. The different drummer's beat they march to can be peppy and cheerful or dramatic and lugubrious, depending on their continuously shifting whims and moods. They thrive on the boundless realm of make-believe and fairy tales. They thrill to live performances.

A few simple rules about proper behavior at public events — with emphasis on the basic adage of making sure their behavior in no way detracts from anyone else's possible enjoyment of the occasion — should be sufficient to prepare even most preschoolers for frequent outings into the world of live performances — theatre, ballet, symphony, circus, opera, puppetry, choral presentations, and more.

Don't stop with our list of possibilities. Check newspaper and magazine listings weekly for current shows by local companies as well as traveling productions. Ordinary children's movies and plays are not the only sources of artistic stimulation; be daring in your choices, and let your children's imaginations run wild.

We should mention that the Memphis Arts Council is a wonderful umbrella agency that supports through funding, advertising, and other means many of the performing arts sources listed below. The Memphis Arts Council also helps enable the production and exhibition of visual arts in our city.

DANCE

DANCE WORKS
414 S. Main
Memphis, Tennessee • 452-8811

Originated for disadvantaged children ages 7 and older, this inner-city dance company offers school-year and summer training programs for young dancers. (The $2 per class fee is only a fraction of the normal dance lesson fee. Students must establish financial-need eligibility.) Public shows lasting about 1 1/2 hours are offered in December and May (tickets are free!). Guest artists often perform with the children in the professional-caliber shows. With a classical ballet foundation laid first, the dancers are encouraged to experiment with ethnic and international dances. They also receive instruction in nutrition and other health topics.

MEMPHIS CONCERT BALLET
4569 Summer Avenue
Memphis, Tennessee • 763-0139

Offering classes for 5-year-olds through high school students by semester, Memphis Concert Ballet trains in classical ballet. The October-April season includes four season performances in the magnificent Orpheum Theatre Downtown — one show always being _The Nutcracker_ in December. Extras are used in all the professional concerts, and the children studying at the Summer Avenue studio are often among the crew of extras. Memphis Concert Ballet also provides touring shows for the tri-state area, including inner-city schools in Memphis. Discounted tickets for all shows are available to students.

MEMPHIS DANCE ALLIANCE
452-8811

Memphis Dance Alliance is an organization that sponsors two major dance events each year. The last Saturday in April is the culmination of National Dance Week. The alliance produces an all-day "celebration of dance" at Hickory Ridge Mall. Young students from schools all over the area come to show what they've learned during the past year. The alliance also makes possible an annual workshop led by an outstanding guest artist who then performs in a concert that is open to the public.

PROJECT MOTION
324-7534

A "contemporary modern" dance company, Project Motion offers three formal public performances per season (tickets are $7 for adults, $5 for students and senior citizens) ranging from classical jazz to more lyrical pieces to abstract movement pieces and even some dance drama featuring lots of props such as body masks, long pieces of cloth, a table, and chairs. The dancers (ages 20 through 30-something) rehearse at Memphis Concert Ballet's studio. Without a permanent home yet for their public performances, they especially enjoy the space at Brooks Museum of Art, where the January concert is given. In addition to the season performances, Project Motion takes a number of performances each year to local schools and community events like Arts in the Park. Some performances are geared more toward children than others; a quick phone call to Project Motion will let you know whether a particular performance is likely to be too long or serious for little ones.

PYRAMID DANCE COMPANY
5341 Rich Road
Memphis, Tennessee • 682-2476

Specializing in Middle-Eastern dance, the Pyramid Dance Company provides instruction in folk and solo dancing. Although most students are adults, some children take the classes. There are two season performances each year at the Old Daisy Theatre on Beale Street. These festive affairs include dinner. Families, especially those of Middle-Eastern heritage, enjoy the colorful costumes and jewelry of the dancers and the exotic music. Pyramid-trained dancers also perform frequently at community festivals and other events.

RIVER CITY BALLET COMPANY
2016 Pendleton
Memphis, Tennessee • 743-8445

This neo-classical ballet company is composed of young dancers. The training ranges from classical to contemporary and jazz ballet. Two company performances a year are held at Memphis State University in the Music Auditorium. Guest performers from the Dance Theatre of Harlem have been highlighted at past concerts. The artists from the Harlem Theatre also work with the River City Ballet Company students, some of whom have received full scholarships to study in Harlem. The 1991-92 schedule includes *The Wizard of Oz* in December and a pops concert in the spring.

FOLK AND OTHER DANCING

A number of private dance studios offer instruction in clogging, square dance, tap, and other versatile forms of the art of dance. Body movement in rhythm with music is fun for all ages. Watch newspaper listings for classes offered to children as well as adults, or call local youth organizations or religious organizations to inquire about what is available. To find out where you might see performances by the **Cottontown Cloggers**, a traditional southern Appalachian free-style clogging group with loads of energy, call Roger Maness at 725-4165. (The Cottontown Cloggers perform annually at the Pink Palace Arts and Crafts Fair in addition to their frequent performances for other events by request.)

MUSIC

BEETHOVEN CLUB
263 S. McLean at Peabody (across from the library)
Memphis, Tennessee • 274-2504

Founded in 1888 by Martha Trudeau, the Beethoven Club sets out to stimulate musical interest in the Memphis area and develop talent in its members. Two of its four groups, the Senior Department and the Performers, make available to the public annual performances that sometimes feature international artists. The Beethoven Club's remaining groups are the Musical Arts Group and the Vivace Junior Group. Given a French name to reflect their liveliness, the Vivace Group comprises children through the age of 18. It meets monthly on Saturday mornings. The 70 or so talented children in the club support and encourage one another, and they perform regularly for one another (and occasionally for the public, by special request). Dues are $3 per year. Children normally are sponsored for membership by their music teachers, but if you have a talented child, you may want to call the Beethoven Club for more information.

CALVARY FRIENDS OF MUSIC
Calvary Episcopal Church
102 N. Second
Memphis, Tennessee • 522-1808

Calvary Episcopal Church is the setting for lots of beautiful music and other programs to nourish the spirit of the community. Noonday concerts on Wednesdays from the middle of September until the end of January each year feature anything from baroque to jazz, executed by flute, organ, classical guitar, organ, voice, and other instruments. Readings, play excerpts, and other entertainments fill out the series. The concerts are free, and parents are encouraged to bring any children who are still at home with them. (Lunch is available at a cost of $3.50 following the concerts.) Calvary also hosts a concert series that charges an admission on designated Sunday evenings. Call for more information.

CONCERTS INTERNATIONAL
Harris Auditorium
Central Avenue
Memphis State University Music Building • 678-2418

The chamber music offered in this concert series features prominent musicians from all around the world. (The 1991-92 season, for example, presents performers from the Soviet Union, Hungary, and France.) The October-March season includes three or four concerts. Tickets cost around $15-20 per person. Older children with some training in music should enjoy the opportunity to hear great international musicians.

GERMANTOWN COMMUNITY CHORUS
748-1911

Offering three or four major concerts per year (at a variety of locations), this community chorus is open to all adults. Germantown Cumberland Presbyterian Church is the location for weekly rehearsals. Singing sacred music, Broadway show tunes, patriotic music, and just about any other kind of music imaginable, the Germantown Community Chorus concerts should be enjoyable for all family members.

HARBOR TOWN CONCERT SERIES
Settler's Point Pavilion
Mud Island • 527-2770

This weekly jazz series is ideal for families. The free series runs from May through October. Don't forget your blanket and picnic. The series was on Sunday afternoons in 1991, but there will possibly be a change to Monday evenings or some other time of the week in 1992. Take the Auction Street bridge to Mud Island, and turn right to Harbor Town.

JAZZ IN THE PARK SERIES
The Raoul Wallenberg Shell
Overton Park

Sponsored by the Save Our Shell Committee, this jazz music series takes place during one month each year. Drawing from the local jazz community, as well as occasionally bringing in internationally-renowned performers, the series features outdoor concerts for the entire family. Admission varies by concert, usually a few dollars per adult. Children under 12 are admitted free. Watch the newspaper for details.

LINDENWOOD CONCERTS
Lindenwood Christian Church
40 East Parkway South (at Union Avenue)
Memphis, Tennessee • 458-1652

This versatile concert series offers something for everyone — from the serious, heavy tones of classical music to the pop strains of the Christmas

Spectacular. About eight concerts make up the regular September-May season each year. At least one show is directed especially toward children, often with children as performers. Sporadically (about once every two years) special children's matinees are offered to area schools, with such features as organ or percussion demonstrations. Although concerts require advance tickets because of the reserved seating, three of the concerts are free to the public. Other concerts require a donation of $8 per person. (Group special dispensations, including some discounts, are available.) Most concerts are evening performances; a few take place on Sunday afternoon. A nursery is available for small children. Call 458-1652 for guidance on which concerts are likely to be of greatest interest to children.

MEMPHIS BOYCHOIR
St. John's Episcopal Church
322 S. Greer
Memphis, Tennessee • 323-8597

The three-year-old Memphis Boychoir has already released two recordings. Boys in fourth-seventh grades can audition for the choir. After extensive rehearsals, they give occasional public performances in Memphis and on tour. The songs they sing include both sacred and secular music from that written in the present all the way back to the 16th century.

MEMPHIS IN MAY INTERNATIONAL FESTIVAL, INC.
525-4611

This month-long annual celebration of Memphis and an honored country features entertainment of all types. Two of the most popular events are the Beale Street Music Festival and the classic Sunset Symphony on the Mississippi River. Picnics and blankets are in order!

MEMPHIS STATE UNIVERSITY MUSIC DEPARTMENT
Music Building
Central Avenue • 678-2541

The Memphis State University Music Department offers a wonderfully diverse program of music to the community. Many of the performances are free; some charge a modest admission fee. A few of the regular annual offerings include concerts by the University Orchestra, Sound Fuzion (students who sing popular music from the '40s, '50s, and '60s primarily), University Singers, MSU Oratorio, and the MSU Symphonic Band. The spring New Music Festival appeals to composers and others interested in very modern music. MSU Jazz Week is also celebrated in the spring. For a complete listing of the public musical events available at Memphis State, call 678-2541 or write to the Music Department, MSU, Memphis, TN 38152.

MEMPHIS SYMPHONY ORCHESTRA
3100 Walnut Grove Road
Memphis, Tennessee • 324-3627

Memphis's big-time symphony orchestra does our city proud! Conductor Alan Balter and the musicians he directs are top-notch performers. With a regular season consisting of beautifully executed classical symphonic music as well as sprinklings of pops and other special renditions, the symphony brings in guest soloists of international renown — pianists, flutists, violinists, cellists, baritones, and more. Most regular season concerts take place Downtown at the Vincent de Frank Music Hall, located at Poplar Avenue and Mid America Mall. But this versatile orchestra also regularly transports its glorious strains to such delightful locations as Dixon Gardens, the banks of the Mississippi River, The Peabody, area schools, and many other places. Tickets generally range from $10 to $23, with 50-percent student discounts. Season subscriptions are available.

MEMPHIS TRADITIONAL JAZZ FESTIVAL
753-5556

Taking place the first weekend of October in downtown Memphis (exact future location undetermined as of this writing), the Traditional Jazz Festival features all forms of jazz music — Dixieland, blues, ragtime. The individual tickets, at upwards of $20, are somewhat prohibitive for most families with children, but it is hoped by the organizers that they can offer at least one free performance per festival in coming years.

RIVER CITY COMMUNITY BAND
678-3201

Fifty-sixty local musicians (hobbyists, not professionals) make up the River City Community Band. Their regular series includes about six outdoor concerts at Memphis Botanic Garden and one free performance at the Mid-South Fair. The doctors, lawyers, teachers, and other community members who make up the volunteer band also give several shows each year as a public service for retirement groups and others. A real potpourri of music issues forth from the River City Band — marches, patriotic songs, Broadway music, and more. Families are encouraged to bring a blanket and a picnic to any of their outdoor concerts. Check local news listings for times and places.

SUNDAY GOSPEL SERENADE
Handy Park • 525-4606

Hosted by the Watson Family Singers, this Sunday afternoon concert series begins on Mother's Day in May and runs through the end of October, with serenades filling the park with music and "promoting unity" within the community from 3:30 till 6:00 p.m. The wide variety of musicians participating includes choirs, soloists, ensembles, and even a few walk-ons. All races and nationalities are represented, giving the event an interesting international, gospel flavor. Guests have visited from as far away as Germany, China, and New Zealand. Donations are gratefully accepted at the free concerts.

OPERA

OPERA MEMPHIS
678-2706

Grand opera is SPECTACLE. And who loves a showy exhibition more than children! The colorful, ornate costumes; the booming voices; the swelling of the orchestra; the dramatic action — the elements of opera are irresistible to children given the opportunity to enjoy the musical extravagance. In its four-concert series (running from October to May), 36-year-old Opera Memphis presents one musical theatre piece each year *(Porgy and Bess* in 1991). This might be the performance to launch children into their opera experience, working up to the elaborate Italian productions. Opera nights are Saturdays (at 8 p.m.) and Tuesdays (at 7:30 p.m.). Even grade-school children (if they can stay awake late enough) should have a "grand old time" at the opera.

MEMPHIS STATE UNIVERSITY MUSIC DEPARTMENT: OPERA THEATRE
Music Building
Central Avenue
Memphis State University • 678-3768

This university-centered opera group offers at least one performance per semester.

THEATRE

BLUES CITY CULTURAL CENTER
525-3031

Local and regional playwrights supply the original works for the Blues City Cultural Center, which seeks to expose and explore "the Southern experience." The four-production season runs from September through June, with shows given at the LeMoyne-Owen Little Theatre, 807 Walker. Although the current season is directed to an adult audience, the Cultural Center generally provides some family fare. Creative arts classes are offered to young people on Saturdays at the Theatre Works building, 414 S. Main; the students' efforts culminate in a holiday play for families. The company also takes on tour eight shows for families and youth.

CIRCUIT PLAYHOUSE
1705 Poplar Avenue
Memphis, Tennessee • 726-5523

Closely allied with Playhouse on the Square, Circuit Playhouse is located in a renovated old movie theatre (formerly the Evergreen) at the corner of Poplar and Belvedere. Of the two theatres, Circuit provides more of the off-Broadway, avant-garde shows. Seating only 140 patrons, Circuit Playhouse gives the audience a sense of intimacy with the performers. The annual holiday production of *The Lion, the Witch, and the Wardrobe* is a local favorite. Many of the other shows in the eight-production season are suitable for children as well. (Playhouse on the Square season tickets may be used at Circuit Playhouse. See the Playhouse on the Square listing below for more information.)

GERMANTOWN CHILDREN'S THEATRE
7771 Old Poplar Pike
Germantown, Tennessee • 757-7382

With their own theatre and stage (other amenities in the works), children in the Germantown area have a working space suitable for fostering their budding theatrical skills. The theatre is in the Arts Building across from the Pickering Building in C.O. Franklin Park. Auditions are held for the six varied productions each year. Each production involves nightly rehearsals until opening night, then a total of seven shows for public viewing (at $2 per general admission ticket). Children are in charge of all aspects of the productions, including the technical areas of lighting and sound, with the assistance of an adult director. Participating children range from 4 or 5 years old to 18.

GERMANTOWN COMMUNITY THEATRE
3037 Forest Hill Road
Germantown, Tennessee 38138 • 754-2680

Housed in a turn-of-the-century brick one-room schoolhouse, the Germantown Community Theatre offers more of interest than just its unusual, intimate building. The regular season includes a full plate of popular Broadway hits, as well as the recent addition of some classics

(1992 promises Shakespeare's *The Taming of the Shrew*). The annual holiday presentation, which plays to a packed house each night of its nearly-month-long run, is *The Best Christmas Pageant Ever*. Dozens of auditioning kids get to perform in this holiday treat. Most of the selections at Germantown Community Theatre are quite enjoyable for the entire family.

HARRELL PERFORMING ARTS THEATRE
440 W. Powell Road
Collierville, Tennessee 38017 • 853-3228

This fairly new theatre in nearby Collierville chooses a very family-oriented series of theatre pieces each year. Universal appeal is its goal. Children have roles in most performances at the theatre. The 1991-92 season reads like a high school literature syllabus, with such offerings as *Legend of Sleepy Hollow, The Nutcracker, Little Women, Anne of Green Gables,* and *Tom Sawyer.* The theatre is not necessarily committed to the classics forever, but it is committed to family fare.

LITTLE THEATRE
Theatre Memphis
630 Perkins Rd. Exit
Memphis, Tennessee • 682-8323

This auxiliary of Theatre Memphis (see listing below) offers more experimental or alternative pieces than its parent theatre. Little Theatre occupies its own little "black box" area of the building on Perkins. You may want to call ahead for guidance on appropriate ages for audience if you are not sure about a particular play.

McCOY THEATRE
Rhodes College
2000 North Parkway
Memphis, Tennessee 38112 • 726-3838

This intimate "black box" theatre is very versatile. (Its seats and stage are moveable so that it can expand or contract as required by its current production.) The October-May season includes one musical production, one classical production (such as a Shakespeare play), and two other plays. The cast is made up of Rhodes students, community members, children, high school students, and others. The company production in the spring is done entirely by students — set design, lighting, directing, costumes, the works! — who are graded on their efforts. This show is free, but the other productions do have an admission charge. The theatre also hosts other events, including a benefit concert highlighting one artist in the spring.

MEMPHIS CHILDREN'S THEATRE
2635 Avery
Memphis, Tennessee • 452-3968

Any theatre devoted to productions entirely focused towards children's interests and talents is likely to hold some real surprises. This one, founded by Lucille Ewing for children ages 5-18 and housed in its own Park Commission building, is no exception. Memphis Children's Theatre gives youngsters experience in all facets of theatre production — from acting and directing to taking care of the behind-the-scenes and technical aspects of the shows. Subject matter can range from hilarious enactments of Dr. Seuss' rhythmical stories to presentations of Chekhov short stories or classic fairy tales to super-charged dance concerts. A Young Playwright's competition also showcases the talents of a local young writer each year. Auditions are held regularly. Watch news announcements if your child is interested in getting involved in the world of theatre. Tickets for the shows are nominally priced.

MEMPHIS JEWISH COMMUNITY CENTER THEATRE
6560 Poplar Avenue
Memphis, Tennessee • 761-0810

Offering at its Centerstage popular musicals, dramas, and comedies, Memphis Jewish Community Center also provides a worthwhile family entertainment series featuring such attractions as family-oriented concerts. Open to the public. Call for more information.

MEMPHIS STATE UNIVERSITY THEATRE
3745 Central Avenue
Memphis, Tennessee • 678-2565

With both a Mainstage and a Studio, MSU Theatre offers an interesting variety of dramatic, musical, and lyrical presentations open to the public. Many are suitable for children. Call ahead for guidance.

THE ORPHEUM
203 S. Main
Memphis, Tennessee 38103 • 525-3000

This "grand old opera" house hosts an outstanding series of Broadway touring shows. More expensive than local productions, the ticket prices reflect the cost of fabulous productions by national touring companies. (For more information see listing in Chapter 1.)

PLAYHOUSE ON THE SQUARE
51 S. Cooper
Memphis, Tennessee 38104 • 725-0776

Housed in a converted movie theatre (formerly the Memphian) like its companion theatre, Circuit Playhouse, Playhouse on the Square is near Overton Square, a popular dining and entertainment district in midtown Memphis. Alternating *Peter Pan* and *Annie* as the family-oriented Christmas holiday production, the theatre caters to sell-out crowds in either year. Playhouse on the Square presents more conventional shows than Circuit, many of them geared toward families or especially directed toward children, like the popular presentations in the past of *Charlotte's Web* and *The Pied Piper*. Both theatres feature opening night parties, touring school performances, special classes for children and adults, and a youth conservatory in the summer. The conservatory is offered to aspiring performers aged 6-17, with a public performance at the end of the two summer sessions (three weeks each for the senior group, two weeks each for the juniors — under age 12). Playhouse on the Square is a small theatre, and, like Circuit Playhouse, presents a variety of musicals, comedies, and dramas. (Season subscriptions may be used at either of the two theatres.)

THEATRE MEMPHIS
630 Perkins Extended
Memphis, Tennessee • 682-8323

Applauded for its perennial holiday production of the Dickens classic *A Christmas Carol,* Theatre Memphis is one of the major centers of theatrical activity in the area. Located in a modern facility in east Memphis, the company offers in its Mainstage auditorium a full season of well-produced conventional theatre pieces, including musicals, comedies, and dramas. Often lighthearted and amusing, the plays are usually appealing to the entire family.

THEATRE WORKS
414 S. Main
Memphis, Tennessee 38103 • 525-2887

Providing space for a number of other creative arts organizations, Theatre Works offers at its small downtown theatre quite experimental, often original, plays that would have a hard time finding a home elsewhere. Some of the productions are excellent. Much of the material is adult in nature. A call to the theatre should clarify the suitability level for younger viewers.

OTHER THEATRES AND COMPANIES

There are other locations and groups in the Memphis area that offer occasional family entertainments. Some have no permanent home or set schedule, so watch news listings for items of interest to your family. Names to watch for include **Bartlett Community Theatre, Frayser-Raleigh Community Theatre, Christian Brothers University,** and **Shelby State Community College Theatre.**

OTHER PERFORMING ARTS

JIMMY CROSTHWAIT PUPPETRY
867-8100

Jimmy Crosthwait is well-known in the Memphis area as the creator and manipulator of a cast of "real characters" in the guise of puppets. His puppets perform frequently at the Memphis Pink Palace Museum for school groups and occasionally for the general public. Families interested in puppetry can hire out Crosthwait and his crew of sharp-tongued bouncing figures by calling him at the above number.

SHRINE CIRCUS
5770 Shelby Oaks Drive
Memphis, Tennessee • 377-7337

What better represents pure entertainment to any child than the circus! The local Shrine Temple sponsors an annual three-ring affair (usually at the Mid-South Coliseum) in March or April. George Coronas and Tarzan Zerbini are two of the producers who have been commissioned in previous years to bring their special brands of sawdust excitement to the children of Memphis. Swaying poles, trained elephants and tigers, trapeze artists, and dancing dogs are just a few of the acts spectators can expect to enthrall them each year at the Shrine Circus. 1992 ticket prices of $5-$9 include parking. Morning performances for school groups cost $1.50 per show. The Shriners also give away about 13,000 free tickets to handicapped and underprivileged children.

RINGLING BROTHERS/BARNUM & BAILEY CIRCUS

The BIG one usually makes an annual appearance in Memphis, too. Watch for newspaper, TV, and radio announcements heralding its arrival. (One year the circus was late arriving in town. Our family's opening night tickets ended up including the unexpected treat of a royal entertainment by the circus hands and stars while they were assembling the works. It made for a late night, but one fondly remembered for years to come.)

NATIONAL TOURING SHOWS

Sesame Street Live, Ice Capades, and other national touring shows. Lots of wonderful traveling shows come to Memphis. Keep an eye open and an ear out for news of shows your family will enjoy.

ASSORTED OTHER SHOWS

A number of organizations in the Memphis area that are hard to pin down offer excellent, highly unusual entertainment for families. Pay attention to current news releases on the activities of such groups as **The Mediaeval Knights of Anachronism** and **The Red Balloon Players.**

5. Sports and Recreation

It's an indisputable fact that children love to be active, whether indoors or out. Movement is essential! Unfortunately, far too many children spend endless hours passively staring at the television set or—more recently—glued to a chair in front of a computer game. Schools have had to trim physical education programs in the era of budget cutbacks, and daily recesses have been shortened. Parents can make a difference by becoming actively involved in their children's athletic and physical development.

If your family is not already involved in a regular family athletic activity, start "selecting and sampling" some of the sports we have listed. We hope you find a few that your whole family can enjoy together. We know you'll have fun looking!

SPECTATOR SPORTS

MAJOR LEAGUE SPORTS

Memphis Chicks (Southern Baseball League, Class AA). Games are held at Tim McCarver Stadium from April through September. The Chicks are the farm club of the Kansas City Royals. Bo Jackson got his professional baseball start with the Chicks in 1986. There are approximately 70 home games. For information call 272-1687.

U.S.A. Baseball (Olympic Team and Training Site). Training and playing every year, including Olympic years, the U.S.A. Baseball Team plays between 10 and 20 home ballgames against international teams, including Cuba and Korea. The season runs from June through July. Games are held at Millington Legion Field (also known as U.S.A. Stadium), located just outside Memphis off Highway 51 on the way to Millington. An official Olympic Training Center Gift Shop is also on the site. Call 872-7228 for training and game schedules, along with gift shop hours.

ON THE HORIZON

NFL Football. Memphis has applied for and is hopeful of receiving a National Football League franchise. A decision is to be made in 1992, so watch for further details.

COLLEGIATE SPORTS

Memphis State University Tiger Basketball (Great Midwest Conference, Division I). Games are held at The Pyramid from November through March. For information call 678-2331.

Memphis State University Tiger Football (Independent, Division I). Games are held at Liberty Bowl Memorial Stadium from September through December. For information call 678-2331.

Memphis State University—Other Sports. Call 678-2331 for information and schedules.

Rhodes College Lynx Basketball (NCAA, Division III). Games are held at Mallory Gym from November through February. For information call 726-3954.

Rhodes College Lynx Football (NCAA, Division III). Games are held at Fargason Field from September through November. For information call 726-3954.

Rhodes College—Other Sports. Call 726-3954 for schedules and information.

Other College Sports. There are many other colleges and universities in the Mid-South area that have athletic games open to the public. Here are the phone numbers of just a few if you are interested in their schedules: **Christian Brothers University,** 722-0370; **Shelby State Community College,** 528-6754; and **LeMoyne-Owen College** (basketball), 942-7323.

Liberty Bowl Memorial Football Game. Played in late December, this popular college bowl game is played at the Liberty Bowl Stadium, where one of the armed forces teams (Army, Navy) is paired off against one of the top-ranked college teams. Call 767-7700 for information.

AUTO RACING

Memphis International Motorsports Park. Just one mile north of the city limits at 5500 Taylor Forge Road 38053, this 600-acre park features a three-eighths-mile clay oval, an eighth-mile oval, a quarter-mile drag strip, and a two-mile road course. Some regularly scheduled events include WERA Formula USA Grand Prix Motorcycle Road Racing, NHRA Firestone/TNN E.T. Series, NHRA Winston Drag Racing, and Sports Car Club of America Concours d'Elegance Rally. For schedules and information call 358-7223. Open March-October. (Children 12 and under admitted free to most events with paying adult.)

BICYCLE RACING

A variety of events is scheduled throughout the year for bicycle enthusiasts—riders and spectators alike. Races to benefit various charities are held almost every month. The Memphis Hightailers Bicycle Club prints a monthly newsletter, *The Tailwind*, listing all bicycling opportunities. You can pick up a copy at most area bike stores.

The **Memphis in May Triathlon,** featuring swimming, bicycling, and running, is becoming a popular event for not only regional athletes, but many national and international competitors as well. Call 525-4611 for information. The Sunday edition of *The Commercial Appeal* also lists upcoming sports events in the column titled "Events Datebook."

GOLF

Federal Express-St. Jude Golf Classic. Held in late June at the Tournament Players Club at Southwind Golf Course, this week-long event includes a Classic Pro-Am and a Celebrity Pro-Am, along with first-, second-, third-, fourth-, and final-round play by top-ranked golfers. For information call 748-0534.

HORSE SHOWS AND RODEOS

Memphis is fortunate to have an extensive equestrian population with many riding events being held each year. The neighboring city of Germantown is known throughout the country for its fine competitions and shows featuring the best of the regional and national riders. Among the most popular events held every year are:

Germantown Charity Horse Show. Featuring multi-breed horses including the famed Tennessee walking horse, this event is held the first part of June at the Germantown Charity Horse Show Ground. For information call Bess Barry at 754-7443.

Memphis Hunter-Jumper Classic. Held in June at Showplace Arena located at the Agricenter. For information call 756-7433.

Mid-South Fair Rodeo. Held during the Mid-South Fair at the end of September. Located at the Mid-South Coliseum. Call 274-3982 for information.

Mid-South Quarter Horse Breeder Futurity. An annual event held at Showplace Arena. Call 756-7433 for information.

Liberty Bowl Rodeo. Showplace Arena also hosts this action-packed rodeo at the facility in the Agricenter. Held in December. Call 756-7433 for information.

Many additional equestrian events are held at the Germantown Charity Horse Show Grounds and the Showplace Arena (numbers listed above). For more information you may call the **West Tennessee Hunter Jumper Association** at 754-1661, **Southern Amateur Saddle Club** at 876-5511, **American Quarter Horse Association** at 382-2573, or **Mid-South Quarter Horse Breeders** at 853-0350.

RUNNING

First Tennessee Memphis Marathon. Held in early December, the Memphis Marathon is becoming a favorite of national and international competitors. This race is sanctioned by the Road Runners Club of America (RRCA) and in 1991 was designated as the Tennessee State Marathon Championship. For information call 523-4726 or 800-489-4040, Ext. 4726.

TENNIS

International Indoor Tennis Tournament. The world's finest tennis players compete in one of the most prestigious tour events of the year. Held in mid-February at the Racquet Club of Memphis. For information call 765-4400.

INDIVIDUAL, FAMILY, AND TEAM SPORTS

ARCHERY

There are several locations in the Memphis area to enjoy archery. T.O. Fuller State Park (see listing in Chapter 2) has 14 practice and 28 tournament targets spread over a 20-acre range. Contact your local archery store listed in the *Yellow Pages* under **Archery Equipment & Supplies** and **Archery Ranges** for information in your area concerning lessons and competitions.

BADMINTON

Not only is badminton great fun, but it also develops hand-eye coordination and speed. The equipment is not expensive and can be set up in your yard if you have the space. If not, the equipment can easily be transported to a park. Badminton can be played at almost any age level by adjusting the net, and injuries are almost non-existent because the playing surface is grass. The game can be easy-going, but the more skilled player will be surprised to discover how vigorous and competitive it can be.

BALLOONING

Hot air balloons are fascinatingly beautiful to the youngest child . . . and the oldest adult. If you are interested in a ride, you can gather information by looking under **Balloons—Manned** in the *Yellow Pages.*

BASEBALL AND T-BALL

Contact your city or county department of parks and recreation, your area religious organizations, YMCAs, YWCAs, and other groups listed below in this chapter, to locate an association or youth group that has a team for your child to join. Some of these facilities also offer special summer camp programs. (See "Summer Sports Camps" described later in this chapter.)

BASEBALL BATTING PRACTICE

There are a few **Baseball Batting Ranges** listed in the Yellow Pages. Most are open daily March-December. For a modest fee you can practice hitting all speeds and difficulties of pitches.

BASKETBALL

Contact your city or county Department of Parks and Recreation, your area's religious organizations, YMCA, YWCA, and other groups listed below in this chapter to locate an association or group that has a team for your child to join. Some of the facilities also offer special summer camp programs. (See "Summer Sports Camps" listed later in this chapter.)

BICYCLING

Bicycling is a great family activity that offers the cyclist the added benefit of great exercise while enjoying the great out-of-doors. Most city and state parks in the area have designated, well-marked bike paths. (Bicycles may be rented from 8 a.m. to 5 p.m. daily at Meeman-Shelby State Park for $2 per hour.) Several area bike clubs have both weekly rides, social rides, and faster-paced rides scheduled regularly. The **Memphis Hightailers Bicycling Club**, P.O. Box 111195, Memphis, Tennessee 38111, is a good source of information for those looking for programs, rides, and tours. Area bike shops usually have information on upcoming events also.

185

BOWLING

Bowling is one of those rare participation sports that the whole family can join in on regardless of skill level. It can be just as challenging and enjoyable for parents as for the kids, and it can take place in a non-competitive framework. There are numerous bowling lanes in the Memphis area and many that have leagues for children. (Bowling balls come as light as six pounds and can be used by children as young as 3.) For more information, call or go to your nearby lanes listed under **Bowling** in the *Yellow Pages.*

BOXING

The **Police Youth Boxing Club**, 243 Winchester, Memphis, TN 38103 (528-2086) provides boxing, training workouts, and exhibitions for boys 10 and over.

FISHING

Tennessee state law requires all boaters to wear Coast Guard-approved life jackets. Note that a fishing license is required for freshwater fishing in Tennessee for everyone over the age of 13 years. Call the Conservation Board at 325-5840 or the Wildlife Resource Center at 800-372-3928 for more information about licenses.

Fishing is permitted in all streams, lakes and ponds unless otherwise indicated. The Tennessee Tourist Development Office (P.O. Box 23170, Nashville, TN 37202) publishes a brochure "Tennessee Fishing" that lists popular fishing spots and best-catching times for all of Tennessee, including Herb Parsons Lake and Pickwick Lake, both close to Memphis.

There is a wide variety of lakes and rivers for fishing, as well as a variety of fish to catch: crappie, bluegill, white bass, catfish, yellow bass, yellow perch, and pickerel, to name a few. Within Memphis you can fish at:

Agricenter International. (See listing in Chapter 2) The lake is stocked with catfish, and no license is required. The fee is $1 for age 10 and up, free for children 9 and under, and $1.75 per pound of catfish. Call 755-9255 for information.

Audubon Lake. (See listing in Chapter 2.) Fishing in this lake is permitted for children under 16 and senior citizens (age 65 and over). No license is required. An annual fishing rodeo is held here each June for children. Call the parks and recreation department at 325-5741 for information.

Meeman-Shelby State Park. (See listing in Chapter 2.) Poplar Tree Lake is a 125-acre lake equipped with pier, rental jonboats, and boat launch (electric motors only, gas motors not permitted). Fishing is said to be good, even from the bank, for bream, catfish, and large-mouth bass. A Tennessee fishing license is required.

For the child or novice angler, the first fishing trips should be kept simple. You may want to purchase a cheap pre-packaged spincast rod and reel outfit (about $15) that has everything you will need except bait. Pick up some crickets, a box of worms, and maybe a few dozen minnows to add interest. Bank fishing is a safe way to introduce very young children to fishing, but most children would be thrilled to have an opportunity to go out in a boat, even if no fish were caught. Picnicking is a great way to make the time go by when the fish aren't biting, so don't forget to pack some human food, too. Life vests, hats, insect repellent, and sunscreen are also a must for the well-planned fishing expedition.

FOOTBALL

Contact your city or county department of parks and recreation, area religious organizations, YMCA, YWCA, and other groups (listed below in this chapter) to locate an association or group that has a team for your child. Some of these facilities also offer special summer camp programs. (See "Summer Sports Camps.")

GOLF

Golf is a popular sport throughout the country, and Memphis is not to be outdone. There are many junior tournaments sponsored by the Memphis park commission located at many of the over 10 local public courses. *The Commercial Appeal* lists upcoming golfing events in the "Events Datebook" column of the Sunday *Sports* section. Contact the park commission for information concerning summer youth competition at the ranges.

There are over five golf practice ranges listed in the Yellow Pages, some of which offer golf lessons. Three miniature golf courses, **PUTT-PUTT Golf and Games** at 5484 Summer (386-2992), **PUTT-PUTT Golf and Games** at 5720 Mt. Moriah Road Extended (366-7888), and **Al's Golfhaven Golf Range** at 1884 E. Raines Road (332-9481), offer fun for even the youngest golfer in your family.

GYMNASTICS

Gymnastics is one of the best individual sports to help children build self-confidence, flexibility, agility, and body control. You can find everything from toddler tumbling on up to competitive gymnastics available in Memphis. Memphis State University offers different levels of classes for all ages through its continuing education program. Classes are also offered through religious organizations, YMCA, YWCA, and other groups (listed below in this chapter). For those who are ready and interested, an array of events in competitive gymnastics is available at some of the private gyms in Memphis.

HIKING AND BACKPACKING

With a climate conducive to almost year-round outdoor activity, Memphis has a wealth of hiking trails located both within the city and close by. Children love to be outside, and what better family outing than to pack a picnic and head out in a group on a fine trail! For the more adventurous, backpacking is available. Most state parks have well-marked hiking trails. Here is a list to get you started. All are within an hour's drive. Parks with special backpacking trails have been noted.

TENNESSEE
Meeman-Shelby State Park (876-5201).

Shelby Farms State Park (757-7777).

Big Hill Pond (1-645-3036). Nearest town is Pocahontas; backpacking available.

Ft. Pillow State Park (1-738-5581). Nearest town is Henning; backpacking available.

ARKANSAS

Village Creek State Park (501-238-9406). Nearest town is Wynne.

Lake Poinsett State Park (501-578-2064). Nearest town is Harrisburg.

MISSISSIPPI

Arkabutla (601-562-6261). Nearest town is Hernando; trails are limited.

Sardis (601-563-4531). Nearest town is Sardis; trails are limited.

See other chapters in this book for in-depth descriptions of many of these places.

HOCKEY, ICE

There are more than 100 children—boys and girls, ages 5-18—who participate in the **Southern Youth Hockey League** in Memphis. Divided by ability and age, the kids receive instruction along with competitive play. Each year before registration, usually in September, the league conducts free clinics to see if prospective participants are really interested. The season runs from October through the first of March, with home games being played at the Mall of Memphis Ice Capades Chalet. Some of the competitive teams travel to Atlanta, Nashville, and Huntsville to play. For more information call Dan Mungle at 755-2995.

HORSEBACK RIDING

One of the best equestrian centers in the nation, Memphis affords families the opportunity for both pleasure riding and competitive riding.

Meeman-Shelby State Park and **Shelby Farms** (see Chapter 2) both have stables that rent horses and have miles of beautiful trails to explore. **Memphis State University** offers horseback riding lessons through its continuing education classes each semester. For those wanting something more, English and Western lessons are available at many of the stables listed in the *Yellow Pages* under **Riding Academies** and **Stables.**

Area youth groups also offer lessons or summer camps for young equestrians. Check the youth groups listed at the end of this chapter.

Pony rides are always a big hit at birthday parties and carnivals. There are several pony rental groups that cater to such events. Look for listings in the Yellow Pages under **Carnivals** or **Party Planning Service.**

ICE SKATING

For those who like to get their exercise on ice, Memphis has a large indoor rink located at the Mall of Memphis. **Ice Capades Chalet**, 4451 Mall of Memphis (362-8877), is open Monday-Friday 11 a.m.-5 p.m., with added evening hours on Monday, Tuesday, Thursday, and Friday from 7:30 till 9:30 p.m. Saturday hours are 12:30-9:30 p.m., Sunday 1-5 p.m. (Hours in summer months may vary slightly to accommodate competitive skaters.) The cost for skating is $5 plus $2 skate rental.

KARATE AND OTHER MARTIAL ARTS

Karate involves the development of the whole self—body and spirit. Discipline of the mind and emotions is as important as discipline of the body. Therefore, martial arts develop, among other things, a child's self-confidence, ability to focus and concentrate, and respect for other people. Remember that good karate instructors emphasize the defensive nature of martial arts, and they make this very clear to the students at all times. For schools of martial arts, check the Yellow Pages under **Karate and Other Martial Arts Instruction.** Be sure to observe a class before you enroll your child. Some recreation centers and area religious organizations, as well as youth groups (listed later in this chapter), offer classes also.

ORNITHOLOGY (BIRD-WATCHING)

We are fortunate to have within the Memphis city limits one of the premiere bird sanctuaries in the Mid-South. Birders from as far as 500 miles away train their binoculars on the shallow lagoons and wetlands of the EARTH Complex in order to catch a glimpse of one of the several varieties of birds that visit the area. One of the favorite sights is the black-necked stilt. The best months for viewing are April, May, June, September, and October. (For more information about the EARTH Complex, see the listing in the first section of this chapter.) Excellent bird-watching is available at other local spots, such as Shelby Farms, as well.

PARK COMMISSION

Registering more than 360 baseball teams and 450 basketball teams and directing interested parties to soccer and football teams through area community centers, youth organizations, and religious organizations, the park commission can help you locate a team near you for your child (or yourself). All city championships are handled through the Park Commission. For information call 388-5911.

PISTOL AND RIFLERY

A well-equipped practice range is located at 6791 Walnut Grove inside Shelby Farms. Rifle shooting is $3 per person. Young people ages 10-15 must be supervised by an adult. The age limit for the pistol range is 16. The 36-position shooting facility is staffed by NRA-certified instructors that are available by appointment to aid and teach each shooter. You need to bring along your firearm, ammunition, and ear protection (a must!). Hours are Wednesday, Thursday, and Friday from 8 a.m. till 4 p.m., Saturday 10 a.m.-6 p.m., and Sunday noon-6 p.m. (When the darkness falls earlier in the evening, the range will close earlier.) Call 377-4635 for information.

RAFTING AND CANOEING

The Memphis area offers all boat lovers—from basic landlubbers to nautical experts—the opportunity to try their hand, or shall we say paddle, at canoeing and rafting.

River Safety:

- Tennessee state law requires all people aboard watercraft to wear Coast Guard-approved life jackets.

- Always wear shoes to protect your feet from sharp rocks and shells.

- Do not dive or jump into the water, as it is difficult to see submerged rocks and other objects.

- Secure eyeglasses with string or strap.

- Take no more than two children at a time in a canoe with an adult.

- Take special care of keys.

- Anything to be kept dry should be in a waterproof container. Take along a plastic bag for litter.

- **Bluff City Canoe Club** is an excellent source of information. They publish a newsletter, *Currents,* that you can pick up at outdoor outfitting stores. The newsletter lists upcoming scheduled trips (P.O. Box 40523, Memphis, TN 38104).

One of the closest places to experience canoeing is **Shelby Farms** (753-2542)—only 15-20 minutes from downtown Memphis. It is hard to believe you can raft through a forested stream so close to town. Rent a raft that accommodates up to six people and enjoy the natural beauty of the Wolf River. Take a dip to cool off; then picnic at a sandbar. (After Labor Day raft rentals are available only during the weekends through October.) Hours permit Wednesday-Friday 10 a.m.-5 p.m. departures; Saturday-Sunday 9 a.m.-5 p.m. departures.

There are numerous rivers and lakes within one to three hours of Memphis for those who want to make a day of it.

ROLLER SKATING

There are several roller rinks listed in the Memphis Yellow Pages under **Skating Rinks.** Don't forget that roller skating birthday parties are loads of fun for school-age children, and most rinks offer special programs along with group rates for such occasions. Some of the rinks set aside times for younger children to have the rink to themselves while older sisters and brothers are in school. This restricted time for little ones allows them to get the feel of skating without the threat of the bigger kids whizzing by. Check with your nearest rink for special programs, group rates, skate rentals, and availability.

RUNNING

How many of us feel that we are running all day long—here and there, in and out...? There is always a chance in Memphis to put that running "on track." Many Memphis festivals include races as one of the activities, and many non-profit organizations hold annual events. Occasions such as the Fun Run for Families, numerous 5K run/walks, and even the annual Briefcase Boogie provide social structure for the weekend runner. Although not geared for children, the more serious 15K, 30K, and Memphis Marathon excite the strong of heart. **The Memphis Runners Track Club** (278-MRTC) is one local group that is very active in supporting area events. *The Commercial Appeal's* Sunday edition lists upcoming events in its "Events Datebook" found in the *Sports* section.

SCUBA DIVING AND SNORKELING

In Memphis there are several aquatic centers with certified instructors. Although the minimum age for kids to begin scuba diving is 12, most of these centers have snorkeling instruction available also. Find these listed in the *Yellow Pages* under **Diving Instruction** or call 452-DIVE for a special education/activity line that also describes upcoming diving trips.

SKIING

While Memphis is not generally known as a Winter Wonderland, you might be surprised at what is available. **Outdoors, Inc.,** with two locations, 5245 Poplar Avenue, Memphis, TN 38119 (767-6790) and 1710 Union Avenue, Memphis, TN 38104 (722-8988), has information on ski trips and packages. If these trips are just too far and time is too precious, then watch for the **Annual Outdoors, Inc. Cross-Country Ski Race** held at Audubon Park . . . "when it snows." For more information contact the **Memphis Ski Club** at 324-7191.

SKYDIVING

For those who haven't satisfied their desire for the wild blue yonder, there is always skydiving. The age limit for lessons is 18. If an adult in the family or an older child is interested, contact the **West Tennessee Skydiving Association** at 465-DIVE.

SOCCER

According to the Soccer Industry Council of America, only basketball is more popular than soccer among kids under the age of 12. Soccer has mushroomed in popularity all across our country in recent years. It is readily available at recreation centers and churches. Many youth groups also have teams. Children who want serious information about the sport may call the **Tennessee State Soccer Association** at 853-5051. For information on private soccer clubs, see **Soccer Clubs** in the Yellow Pages. Summer soccer camps are held at some of the local colleges and youth organizations. (See "Summer Sports Camps" later in this chapter.)

SPECIAL OLYMPICS

The Tennessee **Special Olympics** organization is very active in the area and can put you in touch with area coordinators. For information on current events, contact their office at 1755 Lynnfield Road, Memphis, TN 38119 (682-5450).

SWIMMING AND AQUATICS

Whether swimming for pleasure or body-toning exercise or practicing maneuvers that could lead to a lifeguard perch, all of us—kids included— need to be "water safe." Local YMCAs, YWCAs, recreation centers, continuing education classes at Memphis State University and Rhodes College, and community pools serving residential areas such as apartment complexes all offer lessons by certified instructors.

There are numerous public pools in Memphis open each summer from mid-June until Labor Day. The usually modest admission varies, depending on the facility and its amenities. Check the city park closest to you to see what is available. (Park Commission number is 325-5759.) Many state parks offer swimming pools, such as the Olympic-size pool at Meeman-Shelby State Park (876-5215). (See Meeman-Shelby listing in Chapter 2.)

Many of the community clubs have swim teams that all member children may join. Memphis State University has an excellent year-round youth swim team for the dedicated swimmer. Whether the top priority is fun or competition varies from program to program. Find out what is involved and decide what you are comfortable with.

Beach-like swimming is available in nearby Olive Branch, Mississippi, at **Maywood Beach** (601-895-2777). Imported beach sand surrounds a huge pool. Acres of adjacent wooded picnic areas make this a good spot for a whole day's outing. (See Maywood Beach listing in Chapter 2 for more information.)

TENNIS

Tennis anyone? Grab a racket and head out the door. The metropolitan area of Memphis is dotted with fuzzy balls and the public and private courts they bounce on. Both indoor and outdoor courts are available. Several public courts are listed below. Most are first-come, first-served; others require reservations and nominal court rental fees.

Bellevue
1310 S. Bellevue Blvd. • 774-7199

Frayser
2907 N. Watkins • 357-5417

Leftwich-Audubon
4145 Southern Ave. • 685-7907 (Indoor and outdoor facilities)

Pierotti-Raleigh
3680 Powers Rd. • 372-2032

Ridgeway
1960 Ridgeway Road • 767-2889

Riverside
435 S. Parkway East • 774-4340

Roark-Whitehaven
1500 Finley Rd. • 332-0546

Wooddale
3391 Castleman • 794-5045

Summer tennis camps for kids are held at area colleges and universities. See the following section, "Summer Sports Camps," for information about available programs.

SUMMER SPORTS CAMPS

In this section, we highlight a few of the many sports camps available in the metropolitan area of Memphis. Many have specialized offerings, and others are more comprehensive sports programs at a particular educational facility. For other programs, be sure to check religious organizations, many of which offer wonderful summer sports camps, and the youth organizations listed at the end of this chapter. The Memphis Public Library publishes a *Summer Survival Kit* that also lists camps around the area. The *Memphis Parent* newspaper, found free around town, usually compiles a list of camps in the area.

CHRISTIAN BROTHERS UNIVERSITY
650 East Parkway South
Memphis, Tennessee 38104 • 722-0370 or 757-9817

Basketball—boys

Divided into grades 4-6 and 7-9, boys get the opportunity to receive individual instruction, daily competition, guest-led clinics, and scrimmages. Camp extras include T-shirt and group insurance. Hours are 9 a.m.-3 p.m.

Basketball—girls

This camp for girls in grades 5-8 and 9-12 offers skill development, scrimmage games, and individual and team fundamentals. The camp features T-shirt and group insurance. Hours are 9 a.m.-4 p.m.

Soccer

Campers age 8 and older (minimum age of 9 for goalkeepers session) learn basic and advanced techniques, which are reinforced in daily games and skill contests. Features include written evaluation, soccer ball, and T-shirt. Hours are 9 a.m.-5 p.m., with overnight camping available.

Volleyball

Conditioning techniques, along with individual instruction and offensive and defensive strategies, are covered in this one-day camp. Sessions are divided for girls in grades 6 through 12. Each session is 3 1/2 hours. Call for further information.

LeMOYNE-OWEN COLLEGE
807 Walker Avenue
Memphis, Tennessee • 942-7323

LeMoyne-Owen usually offers summer sports camps for children. Schedules are set and plans are made each spring. Call in February or March for details.

MEMPHIS STATE UNIVERSITY
Athletics Department
Memphis, Tennessee 38152 • 678-2331

All-Sports Camp

Kids, both boys and girls, ages 6-14, receive instruction in basketball, track, tennis, soccer, and swimming. Recreational games such as volleyball, cricketball, box hockey, and others are also included. Extra features include camp T-shirts, talent shows, ribbons, and awards. Five- and ten-day sessions available. Hours are 8:30 a.m.-3 p.m. Call 678-2315 for details.

Baseball

The Memphis State Baseball Camp stresses fundamentals in hitting, fielding, base running, pitching, and bunting. Sessions are divided by age: Session I, ages 8-10; Session II, ages 11-12; Session III, ages 13-16. Each camper must furnish his own glove, baseball shoes, shirt, and pants. Camp benefits include a T-shirt, hat, and awards for best hitter, defensive player, base runner, and pitcher. The camp begins daily at 8:30 a.m. and concludes at 12:30 p.m. Each session lasts Monday through Friday. Call 678-2452 for more information.

Basketball—boys

Larry Finch, head basketball coach of the M.S.U. Tigers, runs this camp for boys aged 9 and older. Having won 1987 and 1989 Metro Conference Coach of the Year, he heads up a team of coaches who offer a well-rounded program including warm-ups, clinics, team play, films, shooting contests, and swimming. Hours are 8 a.m.-5 p.m., with overnight camping available. Call 678-2346 for more information.

Basketball—girls

Designed to teach basketball fundamentals and improve skills at all levels, this program includes 7-year-old girls through high school seniors. Features include individual coaching and instruction, game strategy, basic fundamentals, films and tapes, and daily games. Camp extras vary but might include T-shirts, speakers, prizes, and evaluation cards. Hours of day camp are 8:30 a.m.-5 p.m., with overnight camping available. Call 678-2315 for more information.

DAE Valley Camp

Held each summer for special children ages 3 and up in an atmosphere of fun and personal attention, the camp is committed to meeting the needs of ALL children. The camp is particularly equipped to meet the needs of special children who are hearing impaired, autistic, learning disabled, hyperactive, motor delayed, physically impaired, or otherwise disabled. Children develop self-confidence, improve small and large muscle coordination, and learn to follow directions through daily activities such as basketball, bowling, group games, skating, gymnastics, tennis, arts and crafts, swimming, trampoline, and much more. Call the Memphis State Continuing Education program at 678-6000 for more information.

Football

Generally catering to boys age 10 through high school, this camp teaches fundamentals and skill positions. It is a non-contact program usually held in June, with hours of 9 a.m.-4 p.m. Much of the program is determined annually, including whether or not overnight camping is available, so call 678-2341 for more information.

Swimming, Tennis, Diving, Canoeing

Offered through the Memphis State University department of continuing education, these sports, among many others, are available each semester. Most classes last six to eight weeks and include children from as young as 6 months (water babies) through adults. Call 678-2381 for information and class schedules.

Continuing Education Program

Although this is not a summer sports camp, we felt it necessary to include information on some of the classes offered all year long, including the summer, through the M.S.U. continuing education department. **Boating safety, sailing, tennis, golf, racquetball, karate,** and **fencing** are all included in the extensive curriculum. Call 678-6000 for information, and watch for the class catalogue inserted in January, May, and August in *The Commercial Appeal.*

Universal Cheerleading Association

The U.C.A. offers a camp covering fundamentals of cheering, tumbling, crowd involvement, partner stunts, and safety. A separate dance camp covers props, pompons, and different styles of dance. Elementary through college-aged students may participate as individual campers, although members of a squad usually participate as a group. Camps normally last four days. Overnight camping is available. Call 387-4300 or 800-238-0286 for more information.

RHODES COLLEGE
2000 North Parkway
Memphis, Tennessee 38112 • 726-3940

Baseball

Boys ages 8 through 14 receive instruction in pitching, catching, infielding, and outfielding fundamentals. Drills involving team defense are also utilized. The camp features two batting cages and a pitching machine. T-shirt is included. Hours are 8 a.m.-noon.

Basketball

This camp offers the chance to work on shooting, dribbling, guard play, rebounding, and passing, along with other fundamentals. For boys ages 8-16, the day will include warm-ups, team games, shooting contests, and swimming. Camp extras include T-shirt and films. Hours are 9 a.m.-4 p.m., with overnight camping available.

Football

Boys ages 8-14 receive instruction for all positions, with emphasis on a positive attitude, teamwork, flexibility, passing and receiving skills, blocking and tackling fundamentals, running, and agility. Use of the Rhodes facility includes practice field, weight room, and pool. T-shirt, films, and lunch are included. Hours are 9 a.m.-5 p.m., with overnight camping available.

Tennis

For even the youngest tennis enthusiasts, this camp offers three hours of individual and group instruction, competition, and an hour of free swim time. Broken down into sessions for 7- to 12-year-olds and 13- to 16-year-olds, the camp is great fun for all. T-shirts and trophies are camp features.

SHELBY STATE COMMUNITY COLLEGE
737 Union Avenue
(Several Additional Campuses Around Town)
Memphis, Tennessee 38104 • 528-6754

Basketball

Shelby State usually offers a summer basketball camp for children. Schedules and plans are made each spring, so call in February or March for details.

RECREATION CENTERS AND YOUTH ORGANIZATIONS

RECREATION CENTERS

Memphis-area recreation centers, run by the city, are an excellent source of activity for children. Some centers might include instruction in such sports as basketball, karate, gymnastics, and tennis, while others will offer swimming, roller skating, and horseshoes. Field trips, puppet shows, arts and crafts, board game competitions (checkers, chess, Scrabble), and drama presentations are found in all centers. The need for after-school care in our nation has not been overlooked, and many of these recreation centers offer after-school programs during the school year. Summer day camps for elementary-aged children are usually offered also. Programs are individualized for each center, and some programs fill up fast, so check early for availability.

The city Recreation Department, a division of the Parks Commission, is responsible for registering over 300 teams during each different "sport season." Many of the youth and religious organizations are teamed through the department. The majority of the coaches for these youth teams are volunteer parents who have either some expertise or some knowledge of the game. Umpires are supplied by the Park Commission to officiate at games. For information on the sports your children wish to play, contact your local recreation department. The staff will provide you with the name and phone number of the person to contact.

City of Bartlett (385-5593 or 385-5594). The Bartlett Recreational Center is located at 7266 Third Road, Bartlett, Tennessee 38135. Featuring activities for all ages, the center also has information about athletic programs for children. For sports information call 385-5592 or 385-5595.

City of Collierville (853-3225). The Community Center, located at 440 W. Powell, Collierville, Tennessee 38107, has activities ranging from athletics to ballet. Call or visit for information.

City of Germantown (757-7375). A wide range of activities is available in our neighboring community, from fitness programs, gymnastics, and basketball to soccer teams, dance, and art classes. Most classes are held at the Germantown Centre at 1801 Exeter. Call to receive a copy of the publication *The Park Bench*, which lists all available activities. The area also has over 15 well-equipped parks that are great for picnics, group games, or just a relaxing afternoon.

City of Horn Lake (393-6178). Many parks and playgrounds are available in Horn Lake, which is just across the border in Mississippi. The Optimist

Club of Horn Lake leases park playing fields each year and sponsors athletic teams. Advertisements in the *Southaven Press* newspaper list sign-up dates.

City of Memphis (325-5753). Memphis has more than 28 recreation and community centers, some with swimming pools, basketball courts, and tennis courts. Most of the centers offer a variety of programs, including athletics and individualized classes. Call for information about facilities and programs.

Shelby County (Conservation Board—325-5840). Packed with parks featuring picnic areas and playgrounds, the county offers plenty of wide-open areas for fun and activity.

YOUTH ORGANIZATIONS

Boy Scouts of America (327-4193). With an emphasis on self-confidence and skill development, the Scouts provide a wide range of activities. Starting with the youngest Tiger Cub at age 6, the progression of levels goes to Cub Scouts, Webelos, and finally Boy Scouts (between the ages of 10 and 17). Arts, science, social skills, and out-of-door activities are mainstays of the program. Weekend camping, sometimes as often as once a month, is a popular and important aspect of the program. Summer camps afford the boys the opportunity to work on badges and individual skills, as well as work with a group. Troops usually meet once a week. Call for information on a troop in your area.

Boys Clubs of Memphis (278-2947). Although the Boys Clubs are part of the nationwide organization called Boys and Girls Clubs of America, each club operates autonomously. Boys from age 7 through high school meet at one of the five different clubs, located mostly in the inner-city area. Basketball, softball, soccer, team handball, mini soccer, flag football, along with arts and crafts, woodworking, science, and computer instruction, are available. Career development and leadership training provide the boys with the opportunity to set goals and obtain them. Programs and times may vary from club to club, but most are open from 2:30-9 p.m. during the school year. There are summer programs for children, including a day camp for children 7-10 and a garden club for teenagers. Call for details on programs available.

4-H Clubs (766-2946). 4-H Club is a youth education program of the Agricultural Extension Service and is open to all youth ages 9-19, regardless of race, color, national origin, sex, or handicap. Utilizing projects to teach life skills, members might be involved with raising a calf, planting trees, or baking bread. Tennessee 4-H programs are designed to build character and self-esteem, develop leadership, and teach life skills. Contact one of the following community clubs for more information:

Arlington Community 4-H Club
Arlington Town Hall
Contact: Ruth Ann Hudson (829-4234)

Bartlett Community 4-H Club
Contact: Alice Darnell (388-8489)

Brunswick Community 4-H Club
Brunswick Headstart Center
Contact: Inez Taylor (388-3433)

Walnut Grove Community Club
Cordova Area
Contact: Sandra Ourth (755-3889)

Whitecaps Community 4-H Club
Collierville Area
Contact: Shirley McLarty (601-895-3692) or Kathy Carver (853-0142)

Girls, Inc. (523-0217). Formerly Girls Clubs of America. With the motto "Growing Up is Serious Business," Girls, Inc. focuses its program on helping girls become responsible and confident adults. Objectives along the way include: sports and adventure, health and safety, careers and life planning, culture and heritage, and self-reliance and life skills. Special features offered are the Adolescent Counseling Center, which provides individual counseling and group workshops, and Project JIFFY, which gives training in job readiness skills. Call the main office number above or one of the centers below for more information on all that is available.

LeMoyne Gardens Center
952 Lenow Mall • 947-6442

Lucille DeVore Tucker Center
600 N. Fourth Street • 526-3791

South Park Center
1568 Robinhood Lane • 743-8062

Girl Scouts of America (767-1440). Girls as young as 5 start their scouting experiences as Daisies, moving on to Brownies (grades 1-3), Juniors (grades 4-6), and Cadettes and Seniors (grades 7-12). The primary goal of scouting is to help girls develop social and practical skills, while learning to appreciate nature and the changing world . . . and to meet and make new friends. Usually meeting once a week, girls may work on badges which represent specific skills, plan and participate in community projects, develop an appreciation for the arts and nature, or prepare for a group camping experience. Summer programs include day camps and overnight camps. For information on the troop nearest you, call 767-1440.

The Salvation Army Boys and Girls Clubs. The Salvation Army offers programs for both boys and girls at the various Corps Community Centers. Adventure Corps, for boys in grades 1-12, divides up the groups into Rangers, Explorers, and Adventurers. Girls are grouped as Sunbeams (grades 1-5) and Guards (grades 6-12). Three Corps Centers are located in Memphis: Winchester Corps Community Center (366-1436), Southside Corps Community Center (525-4980), and Ben Lear Citadel Center (525-3953).

YMCA and **YWCA.** Family memberships are available at a low cost and include reduced fees for programs and special events throughout the year. Additional fees are charged for a wide range of programs that might include:

- Summer day camps
- After-school child care
- Sports lessons (basketball, swimming, soccer, etc.)
- Programs for preschoolers.

We are fortunate to have numerous "Ys" throughout the Memphis area. For the exact location and telephone number of the Y closest to you, call: **YMCA—Administrative Offices** (458-3580) or **YWCA—Central Office** (323-2211).

6. Festivals and Special Events

Memphis loves to party! So do the surrounding towns and communities. Just about any week of the year SOMEONE is celebrating SOMETHING and inviting the city to turn out and join in. All the events we have listed below are open to the public. Many are free; some charge an admission fee. We have tried to give accurate information for each listing, but keep in mind that sponsorships change (or disappear) as interests shift. Don't be disappointed if your most eagerly awaited festival happens to be canceled one year—just look for a new favorite. After all, new festivals are born every day. Celebrate LIFE, and have fun!

JANUARY

Elvis Presley Birthday Tribute. Week surrounding January 8. Many activities planned by Graceland (332-3322) and other area Elvis attractions.

Memphis Boat Show. Held at Cook Convention Center. Hundreds of boats of all types are displayed (576-1200).

Project Motion. Modern dance concert at Memphis Brooks Museum of Art (324-7534).

FEBRUARY

International Indoor Tennis Tournament. Held at the Racquet Club of Memphis. The finest tennis players in the world compete in one of the most prestigious tour events of the year (765-4400).

National Field Trial Championship. Grand Junction, Tennessee. Last two weeks of February. Ames Plantation (1/764-2167) sponsors the competition to determine the national champion bird dog. Visitors may view the action with the mounted gallery.

Black History Month. Special exhibits, programs, and shows at several local galleries, colleges, etc. Center for Southern Folklore (525-3655) is prominent among local celebrators.

Zydeco Festival. Held on historic Beale Street. Features music (526-0110).

All About Kids Show. Spring show—sometime between February and April. Sponsored by the Parenting Center of Memphis and the Junior League of Memphis. Location varies. A combination "parents'/children's convention and trade show" (775-7266).

MARCH

Memphis Mardi Gras on Beale Street. Memphians celebrate "Fat Tuesday" in New Orleans style on the historic Beale Street. Don't forget that Mardi Gras can occur in a different month (526-0110).

St. Patrick's Day at the Magevney House. Docents dress manikins and themselves in special lucky green costumes and invite guests to provide music and other entertainment (526-4464).

Easter Sunrise Service. March or April, depending on where Easter falls on the calendar. A non-denominational service held at Wallenberg Shell in Overton Park (365-7162 or 483-9437).

Pet Week Snapshot Contest. (Sometimes occurs in April.) Sponsored by the Memphis Humane Society (529-2255).

Farm, Home, and Garden Show. Agricenter International (757-7777).

Mid-South Sports Show. Features cars, boat, RVs, and trailers. Takes place at Cook Convention Center (576-1200).

APRIL

Carnival Grand Parade. The floats and bands of this festive parade ushering in the Great River Carnival (formerly the Cotton Carnival) are threatened only by menacing skies or the impish antics of the rascally Boll Weevils (278-0243).

Dr. Martin Luther King, Jr. Memorial March. Commemoration of the contributions of Dr. King to the national struggle for civil rights on the anniversary of his untimely death in Memphis (525-2458).

Memphis Concert Ballet. Spring performance at The Orpheum (763-0139).

Memphis Dance Alliance. Celebration of National Dance Week. Held at Hickory Ridge Mall. Last Saturday in April (452-8811).

Spring Memphis Music Festival. An indoor and outdoor festival on historic Beale Street (526-0110).

Super Chevy Sunday. Features drag races, show cars, hot rods. Held at Memphis Motorsports Park (358-RACE).

International Drag Bike Association Spring Nationals. Drag bikes from all over the world compete at Memphis International Motorsports Park (358-RACE).

Spring Plant Sale. Memphis Botanic Garden (685-1566).

Africa in April. Cultural events include a Festival, a Children's Day, and a Community Day (785-2542).

Memphis Scholastic Chess Tournament. (761-3158).

Skyfest. Sponsored by the Memphis Jaycees. Features hot air balloons, kite show, biathlon (323-8343).

Spring Craft Fair. Jonesboro, Arkansas (501/933-8410).

Holly Springs Pilgrimage. Holly Springs, Mississippi. Tours of historic homes and other interesting buildings. Special luncheons featured (601/252-1530).

Civil War Re-enactment. Holly Springs, Mississippi. Authentic Union and Confederate camps, complete with cannons, at Wall Doxey State Park (601/252-4231).

Taste of Tupelo. Tupelo, Mississippi. State Chili Cook-off (601/844-3768).

World's Biggest Fish Fry. Paris, Tennessee. Includes a rodeo, carnival, and softball tournament (1/642-4707).

─────────────── **MAY** ───────────────

Memphis in May. A month-long salute to a different country each year. Attended by more than a million local, regional, and international visitors. Special events include: the International Barbecue Cooking Contest, Great Wine Race, Beale Street Festival, Sunset Symphony, and Kids Fest. (525-4611). See Chapter 3 listing for additional information.

Dance Works. Spring performance (452-8811).

NHRA Mid-South Nationals. A national Hot Rod Association drag racing competition at Memphis International Motorsports Park (358-RACE).

Cotton Maker's Jubilee. For more than 60 years this tribute to King Cotton includes a midway and the largest African-American parade in the nation (744-1118).

Annesdale-Snowden Historic District Tour. (725-7264 or 726-0173).

River City Junior Tennis Championship. Sponsored by the Memphis Park Commission (325-5755).

Greek Festival. Features authentic Greek meals and pastries, served in a festival atmosphere of music and dance. Many children participate. At the Greek Orthodox Church Annunciation, 573 N. Highland (327-8177).

Fair on the Square. Celebration held on historic town square in Collierville, Tennessee (853-1949).

West Tennessee Strawberry Festival. Humboldt, Tennessee. Parades, recipe contest, pet parade (1/784-1842).

Trenton Teapot Festival. Trenton, Tennessee. View the world's largest collection of antique teapots in Trenton City Hall. Celebration includes street dance, sports activities, arts and crafts, parade, and fireworks (1/855-0979).

Delta Jubilee. Clarksdale, Mississippi. Sports, arts and crafts, rides (601/627-7337).

JUNE

Carnival Memphis. A series of events, exhibits, music, and activities for the entire family, including Memphis Air Show. Features cotton-affiliated "royalty" (278-0243).

Germantown Charity Horse Show. Champion riders compete for trophies, ribbons, and prizes in a four-day national event. Held at the Germantown Charity Horse Show Grounds (385-7075).

Junior Tennis Championships. Sponsored by Memphis Park Commission (362-0232).

Fishing Rodeo. Annual competition for children. Audubon Park (325-5741).

Potter's Guild Spring Show. Held at Grace-St. Luke's Episcopal Church (685-1566).

Native American Intertribal Association Powwow. (276-4741).

The Children's Museum of Memphis Birthday Party. Child-related activities create a fun-filled event (458-2678).

Great Memphis Rubber Ducky Race. Sponsored by United Cerebral Palsy (323-0190).

Pack the Park for LeBonheur. Sponsored by Piggly Wiggly (522-3030).

Galloway Junior Golf Tournament. Sponsored by the Tennessee PGA (725-9905).

Zoo Grass. Food, car show, dancing, and more at the Memphis Zoo (726-9453).

Good Earth Festival. An informative, entertaining celebration at Memphis Botanic Garden (685-1566).

Wynne Farm Festival. Wynne, Arkansas. Music, dancing, and games (501-238-2601).

Razorback Annual Fish Fry. Helena, Arkansas (501/338-8327).

JULY

July Fourth Blues Explosion. A full day of great blues music on Beale Street (527-BLUE).

WMC Star-Spangled Celebration. Downtown comes alive with entertainment and magnificent fireworks (576-7241).

St. Peter's Picnic. Held around the 4th of July at St. Peter's Villa/Home for Children, 1805 Poplar at McLean. Includes carnival games, food, a chili cook-off, and entertainment in an old-fashioned political campaign atmosphere (725-8205).

Libertyland Birthday and 4th of July Celebration. Special activities centering around the amusement park's patriotic theme (274-1776).

Germantown's Family Fourth. Germantown, Tennessee. All-day celebration with fishing rodeo, parade of trikes and bikes, miniature car racing, jugglers, petting zoo, and fireworks (755-1200).

Mid-South Music and Heritage Festival. A two-day event celebrating the ethnic diversity of the South with music, crafts, and food. Held the second week in July at Mid-America Mall in downtown Memphis. Sponsored by the Center for Southern Folklore (525-3655).

Fun in the Sun Jamboree. Sponsored by LeBonheur Hospital (522-3331).

Overton Park Open and the **Audubon Junior Open.** Golf tournaments sponsored by PGA (725-9905).

Kudzu Festival. Holly Springs, Mississippi. Barbecue, entertainment, and a carnival playfully celebrating Mississippi's prolific creeping green vines (601/252-2943).

AUGUST

Choctaw Indian Powwow. Two-day annual powwow held at Chucalissa Archaeological Museum grounds. Spotlights Native American crafts, stickball games, a blowgun contest, and the Green Corn Ceremony (785-3160).

Federal Express/St. Jude Golf Classic. Played at the Tournament Players Club of Southwind, this PGA Tour event benefits St. Jude Children's Research Hospital (748-0534).

Elvis Presley International Tribute Week. Citywide events recognizing Elvis's contributions to the world of music (332-3322).

Elvis: Legacy in Light Laser Concert. Pink Palace Museum and Planetarium (320-6381).

Musical Tribute to Elvis. Libertyland Amusement Park (274-1776).

Elvis Presley International 5K Run. Sponsored by United Cerebral Palsy (323-0190).

Presley Memorial Karate Tournament. Sponsored by LeBonheur Children's Hospital (522-6779).

─────────────── **SEPTEMBER** ───────────────

Memphis Music Festival. A profusion of musical talents filling Beale Street clubs, restaurants, and outdoor stages (526-0110).

Mid-South Fair. Ten tantalizing days of entertainment, exhibits—both rural and urban, contests, concerts, a rodeo, food and games, and a midway. Attracts over half a million people a year (274-8800).

Southern Heritage Classic. Three days of festivities, including an education fair, during the weekend of the Tennessee State vs. Jackson State University football game. Focuses on African-American ethnicity. (Sometimes begins in August.)

Black Family Reunion Celebration. Three-day weekend celebration of the African-American family. Sponsored by the National Council of Negro Women. Highlights a series of pavilions that showcase celebrities, well-known experts on topics of interest, performers, and product promotions (948-5000).

Germantown Festival. All types of arts and crafts spread over 20 acres around Poplar Pike at Franklin-Morgan Woods-Cloyes Park. Antique cars, safety presentations, and pony rides are among the many special features (755-1200).

Recycle Roundup. September-October recycling event sponsored by The Children's Museum of Memphis (458-2678).

Frayser First Festival. Food, entertainment, and arts and crafts set the mood for this community autumn "homecoming." Ed Rice Community Center, 2907 N. Watkins.

VECA Fall Family Festival. Live music, puppet shows, storytelling, and arts and crafts are regular features of this family-oriented celebration of the Vollintine-Evergreen community. Held at St. Therese Catholic Church, 1644 Jackson.

Central Gardens Home Tour. Tour a number of Midtown's finest homes (726-9454).

Greekfest. Traditional Greek food and folk dancing. St. George Greek Orthodox Church, 6984 Highway 70 (527-7536).

Goat Days. Unusual festival in Millington, Tennessee (872-4559).

Informational Seminar for Parents. Parent Training Program sponsored by Memphis City Schools (775-7264).

Dixie Rose Club Fall Rose Show. Memphis Botanic Garden (685-1566).

Rendezvous at the Zoo. Fancy affair at the Memphis Zoo (276-WILD).

Ethnic Food and Arts Festival. Sponsored by the International Heritage Ethnic Festival, Court Square Park, downtown Memphis (576-6000).

Memphis Children's Theatre Carnival. Features games, prizes, and a silent auction (452-3968).

Symphony in the Gardens. The Memphis Symphony plays a concert in Dixon Gardens at 4339 Park Avenue. A marriage made in heaven! (324-3627).

Celebration on the Square: From Bach to Rock. Overton Square (274-0671 or 726-0025).

Cooper-Young Festival. Neighborhood celebration (272-3055).

Calvary Choir Cabaret. Calvary Episcopal Church, 102 N. Second Street (525-6602).

Muscular Dystrophy Telethon. Held at Libertyland Amusement Park (274-1776).

Computer Fair. Open to the public. State Technical Institute, 5983 Macon Road, Memphis (377-4111).

Drug Education and Awareness Conference. Information, exhibits, demonstrations, and more. Sponsored by the Memphis Police Department. Held at Memphis Cook Convention Center (528-2222).

Blues Festival. Holly Springs, Mississippi. Blues, gospel, choral, and fife music (601/252-8000).

OCTOBER

Pink Palace Crafts Fair. One of the largest arts and crafts fairs in the state, with artists and performers. Now held at Audubon Park (454-5600).

Oktoberfest. A salute to autumn with outdoor music, food, arts and crafts in downtown Memphis (526-6840).

Memphis Blues Week. This week-long celebration of the blues features the International Blues Summit and the annual National Blues Awards Show and Jam (527-2583).

Zoo Boo. Everything from palm readers to ghosts to crafts for kids to costume contests. Fun for everyone. Held at the Memphis Zoo (276-WILD).

Arts in the Park. Taking place in Overton Park, this fine arts festival features arts and crafts of all kinds, music and other entertainment, and delectable foods. Second weekend in October (761-1278).

Evergreen Gallimaufry. This neighborhood "hodgepodge" festival includes fine arts, performing arts, good food, and snacks. In midtown Memphis at Evergreen and Poplar (276-0174).

Book and Author Dinner. Friends of Memphis/Shelby County Libraries sponsor this elegant, edifying evening at The Peabody. Six authors discuss their works and lives (727-8852).

Blessing of the Pets Ceremonies. Usually held the first Sunday in October to coincide with the feast day of St. Francis of Assisi. Animals are brought for special blessings. Grace-St. Luke's Episcopal Church, 1270 Peabody (272-7425), and St. Michael's Catholic Church, 3867 Summer (323-0896).

Fall Plant Sale. Memphis Botanic Garden. Features horticultural experts to answer questions (685-1566).

Memphis Belle Classic. Radio-controlled aircraft show over Charles Baker Airport to raise money for restoration of the Memphis Belle World War II bomber (873-3838).

Catfish Cook-off Contest. Music and food, children's rides and a petting zoo. At Agricenter International (528-1970).

Repair Days. The National Ornamental Metal Museum can make a damaged silver tray or worn silver teapot like new (774-6280).

Fall Arts and Crafts Show. Southland Mall, located at Shelby Drive and Elvis Presley Boulevard (346-2773).

Monster Bash. Overton Square (726-0025).

Halloween at the Mallory-Neely House. 652 Adams Avenue (523-1484).

Malloween Magic Festival. Mall of Memphis, 4451 American Way (362-9315).

Memphis Aquarium Show. Oak Court Mall, 4465 Poplar Avenue (682-8928).

Jazz Festival. Sponsored by the Memphis Traditional Jazz Festival, Inc. (576-1200).

Memphis Black Arts Festival. (785-0587).

Farm, Home, and Energy Show. Agricenter International (757-7777).

Subsidium Christmas Carrousel of Shoppes. All kinds of holiday treats from all over the southeastern region of the United States brought together at the Mid-South Coliseum. Benefits the Memphis Oral School for the Deaf (683-6557).

King Biscuit Blues Festival. Helena, Arkansas. Super festival attracts musicians from all around the world (501/338-8327).

NOVEMBER

Mid-South Arts and Crafts Show. Artists and crafts people from two dozen states display their wares at the Memphis Cook Convention Center (363-4178).

Mid-South Square and Round Dance Festival. Local, regional, and national square and round dancers swing their partners in this two-day event at the Memphis Cook Convention Center (363-4178).

Scout Base. Boy Scouts of America, Chickasaw Council, features scout skill demonstrations and activities in a three-day outdoor extravaganza. Takes place at Millington Naval Air Station (327-4193).

Jolly Holly Christmas House. Display of hand-crafted holiday gifts at the Woman's Exchange of Memphis, 88 Racine (327-5681).

Thanksgiving Dinner on Beale Street. Volunteers provide food and labor to share their bounty with the homeless and needy in downtown Memphis on Thanksgiving Day (526-0110).

Folk Art and Craft Show Opening. Center for Southern Folklore opens a special show that runs through February each year. 152 Beale Street (525-3655).

The Peabody Christmas Tree Lighting. In the lobby of the elegant, historic hotel (529-4179).

Holiday Bazaar. Memphis College of Art, Overton Park (726-4085).

Poinsettia Display. Memphis Botanic Garden (685-1566).

Winter Lights. The Memphis Zoo turns on thousands of glittering lights, outlining animal shapes, trees, and more holiday treats. Runs through December (276-WILD).

DECEMBER

Merry Christmas Parade and **Downtown Tree Lighting.** Marching bands and colorful floats are featured in the annual Christmas parade in downtown Memphis, ending at Civic Center Plaza, with the lighting of the official Memphis Christmas tree (526-6840).

Christmas in the City. A variety of activities celebrating the Christmas season in downtown Memphis (526-6840).

City Sidewalks. A citywide holiday promotion by the Convention and Visitors Bureau. Special package offers for holiday visitors to Memphis (576-8181).

Holiday Performing Arts Presentations. Many local theatres and dance companies offer annual presentations of holiday favorites. See listings in Chapter 3 for special holiday productions.

TWIGS Festival of Trees and **Enchanted Forest.** The individually decorated trees are representative of international cultures and local special interests. The Enchanted Forest is a fairyland of animated characters celebrating the season in their own inimitable style. A real treat for everyone in the family. Located at Agricenter International (757-7777).

Maternal Welfare League Christmas House. Children can shop privately for family members (with adult volunteer assistance), have their pictures snapped with Santa, play games, and enjoy other holiday treats. Location changes from year to year.

Memphis Humane Society Holiday Bazaar. You can have your pet's picture made with Santa (529-2255).

Germantown Christmas Parade. Starts at the Germantown Centre and goes to Cameron-Brown Park (755-1200).

Holiday Decoration Show. Memphis Botanic Garden (685-1566).

Christmas Spectacular. Lindenwood Christian Church, 40 East Parkway South at Union Avenue (458-1652).

Holiday Programs at Calvary Episcopal Church. Special December events at this downtown historic church include the Boar's Head Feast and a presentation of Handel's *Messiah*. 102 N. Second (525-6602).

Singing Christmas Tree. Bellevue Baptist Church's melodious "human Christmas tree" offers a gift of music to the community. 2000 Appling Road (385-2000).

Liberty Bowl Football Classic. A nationally televised intercollegiate post-season game at the Liberty Bowl Memorial Stadium. The military service academy represented wins the Commander-in-Chief's Trophy as the host team (767-7700).

7. Day Trips

The three-state area surrounding Memphis and known as the Mid-South is rich in family activities. From nature outings to historical sites to one-of-a-kind manufacturing locations, there is always something interesting to see and do within a couple of hours of home.

We have scouted out and explored a number of these nearby sites for you and described ways you might make them the focus of a single day's occupation. These mini-vacations can provide just the right escape when time is in short supply. One day's car trip will get you to a delightful adventure and back home again, with plenty of time in-between for lots of fun.

We should alert you that you are apt to consider some of our selected cities and attractions rather eccentric. You may wonder why we would recommend an excursion to Grand Junction or Jonesboro or Clarksdale in lieu of describing a tour of Nashville or Little Rock or Vicksburg. Our rationale is threefold. First, distance is a prime consideration. We want you to spend your mini-vacation exploring, not riding in a car. Second, we just bet that you are already fairly familiar with the "classics," as tourist attractions go; you don't need us to tell you that the State Capitol Building is located in Nashville. Third, we want to inspire in you an explorer's sense of adventure when we tell you that we have barely scratched the surface of unique and wonderful, bizarre and fabulous sights to see and things to do right here in your own backyard.

We'll be surprised if you don't come up with your own list of exciting day trips once you get the hang of free-spirited delving into the countryside. In the process you're sure to gain a new appreciation for the peculiar assets of each pocket of the Mid-South. (To get you started, we've listed at the end of this chapter some places to launch your own personalized research.)

Look for the following symbols to help you locate at a glance the particular brand of fun you're looking for at each location.

 NATURE

 SCIENCE

 UNIQUE ATTRACTION

 HISTORY AND GOVERNMENT

 PERFORMING ARTS

 FINE ARTS

COLLIERVILLE, TENNESSEE

Just about half an hour from the heart of Memphis, straight out Highway 57 (Poplar Avenue) sits Collierville, Tennessee. This rapidly growing, yet still friendly, small-ish town takes pride in its ability to balance its strong sense of a colorful history with its pride in forging a dynamic future. The casual traveler heading east out of Memphis on busy Highway 57 is apt to think of Collierville as one more ordinary suburb absorbing the industrial and commercial growth of the ever-expanding nearby city. A right turn down Main Street dispels any such notion.

The old town square, a block south of the highway, is listed with the National Register of Historic Districts; its qualifications for such an honor are immediately apparent. The wooded Confederate Park at the center of the square takes the place of the more familiar courthouse at the heart of other town squares, since Collierville has never been a county seat (either in Tennessee or in Mississippi, the state that laid claim to Collierville until the government surveyors of 1839 re-established the states' boundary line). The park is surrounded by well-preserved red brick buildings of the 19th century, which today house modern commercial enterprises, such as antique shops, gift shops, a drugstore, a general store, a hardware store, and the other components of the basic small town square (as well as the requisite Methodist church dating to 1900).

A bright red Southern Railroad caboose rests on its own private stretch of tracks next to the old depot that now serves as the Collierville Chamber of Commerce. An old stagecoach stop built of logs has been moved to the corner of the park. The parking spaces lining Rowlett Street are often filled during the summer months with the fresh fruits and vegetables brought from neighboring farms to the open-air market.

Try gliding into the 20th century now as smoothly as Collierville itself has done. Go back west on Poplar to Peterson Lake Road, then north to Powell Road, where you'll find the Collierville Community Center (built in 1984) and Harrell Performing Arts Theatre (built in 1987). Offering all the amenities of a modern sports-recreation-entertainment complex, the facilities enable the local folks and their neighbors to approach leisure time seriously.

Community events you'll want to watch for include the arts and crafts Fair on the Square in May, the Sidewalk Stroll sale in September, the Fall Festival featuring crafts and tours of historic homes in October, and the circus in October. For more information, contact the Collierville Area Chamber of Commerce, 125 N. Rowlett, Collierville, TN 38017 (853-1949).

GRAND JUNCTION, TENNESSEE

Drive straight out Highway 57 (Poplar Avenue) from Memphis east to Grand Junction, Tennessee, which is about 50 miles away. (You'll have to make a little dog leg north at Highway 18.) Try to allow time for stops in LaGrange to admire the beautiful old houses and rolling pastures, to read the historic markers, and to gaze at C.L. Pankey's 1892 store, which, sad to say, is no longer open for business.

Grand Junction is a mecca for bird dog lovers from all over the world! The new National Bird Dog Museum (dedicated on February 16, 1991), which is marked by three tall flags and a bronze sculpture of bird dogs and rising quail, is located directly across Highway 57 from Dunn's Inc., a very successful mail-order sporting goods business established in 1950. (Dunn's welcome sign over the front door invites "bird dogs, horse trailers, and muddy boots" — not all inside at once, we presume.) The unusual bird dog museum displays a model of the historic Raines Hotel, which was destroyed by a fire in 1986, in addition to an untold number of portraits of prize-winning dogs and their owners and trainers, lists of champions, National Field Trial trophies and plaques, saddles, and other memorabilia from notable hunts. The museum includes a library devoted to bird dogs and their exploits, and the charming staff will be delighted to school even the least-informed visitors (believe us: we were as uninformed on the subject as they come) on the topic of bird dogs and field trials through newspapers, books, and videotapes. If you want to learn more about creatures with names like Luminary, Flaming Star, Gunsmoke, Lullaby, Hard Cash, and Count Noble, the National Bird Dog Museum is the place for you. Admission is free. There is a small gift shop with items related to bird dogs. Hours are 10 a.m.-5 p.m. Tuesday-Saturday and 1-5 p.m. Sunday.

While you're at the bird dog museum, you'll learn about the National Field Trials that take place every February at Ames Plantation (about two miles from Highway 57—north on Highway 18 and left on Buford Ellington Road). The plantation may be viewed from the road. The home itself is open for public tours on the fourth Thursday of each month from 1-4 p.m. Admission is $2 per person. For more information, call 878-1067.

No visit to Grand Junction is complete without a look at Tennessee Pewter, which recently moved back to its Grand Junction home from a brief tenure in Moscow, Tennessee. (From the museum, continue east on Highway 57 about a block. Turn right on Main Street beside the Junction

Inn Restaurant — a good place for a hearty lunch — and continue straight ahead to the row of buildings. Tennessee Pewter is the tall blue one.) The pewter spinning, casting, and engraving processes can be observed if you arrive on a day when the artist is working (Tuesdays and Wednesdays at the time of our visit). Retail items can also be purchased.

HENNING, TENNESSEE

ALEX HALEY STATE HISTORIC SITE AND MUSEUM

Alex Haley State Historic Site and Museum, 200 S. Church Street at Haley Avenue (1-738-2240). The only state-owned historic site in west Tennessee, the Alex Haley House Museum is the home built in 1919 by Will Palmer, grandfather of *Roots* author Alex Haley, who lived with the Palmers from 1921 to 1929 and for many succeeding summers. The restored home features personal memorabilia from the life and works of Haley, who was inspired by the picturesque town of Henning and by the tales related by his grandparents and aunts to research his ancestors who came to America as slaves and then to write the internationally-popular story of Chicken George, Kunta Kinte, and other Palmer family progenitors. Haley continued to visit Henning frequently up until his untimely death in 1992.

Given the choice of a tape-guided tour or person-guided tour, our group made the right decision. The feisty Henning resident who took us through the house made numerous personal references to her friend Alex Haley as we proceeded room-by-room on our tour. She deepened our appreciation for the man who never abandoned his own roots in quaint Henning in spite of his far-reaching fame. Practically cackling with pleasure— equally over our knowledge of pie safes or our ignorance of Palmer family custom—the delightful tour guide was a treat in herself. Nostalgia items she pointed out that might provide a glimpse into modern history for children born into a highly technological age include an outdoor water pump, a churn, dried peppers, an icebox, a victrola, a coal scuttle, and a spinning wheel.

Less than an hour from Memphis, Henning is a charming little destination, with good home-cooking available at the Just a Small Town Restaurant at 110 North Main. Combine the tour of Henning with a visit to nearby Fort Pillow State Historic area for an A+ day!

• Brochure available.

• Tours are guided—on no particular schedule, just when guests arrive—or tape-directed if preferred.

• Free parking is available on the grounds of the home.

• There is a small gift shop at the entrance offering such items as stationery, pencils, cotton bolls, T-shirts, and Alex Haley books.

• Rest rooms and water fountain available outside the home.

Hours: Tuesday-Saturday, 10 a.m.-5 p.m.; Sunday, 1-5 p.m. Closed Mondays.

Admission: Adults, $2.50; students, $1.

Directions: Follow Hwy. 51 north from Memphis, past Covington, to Hwy. 209. Turn right to Henning. Turn left on Haley Avenue and continue to Church Street.

FORT PILLOW STATE HISTORIC AREA

Fort Pillow State Historic Area, Route #2, Box 109, Henning, Tennessee 38041 (1-738-5581). This beautifully wooded scenic park is named for General Gideon J. Pillow, a Mexican War hero. It was another war, the American Civil War, that took Fort Pillow itself captive. Sitting on Chickasaw Bluff No. 1 overlooking the Mississippi River, Fort Pillow was part of a system of river fortifications. First occupied by the Confederate soldiers, then overtaken by Union troops, it was eventually won back by the Confederacy near the end of the war. The controversial nature of the final battle is documented in a captivating film shown at the park's Interpretive Center. Other displays at the Interpretive Center include Civil War weapons and ammunition, portraits and personal memorabilia, flags, and life-size soldier cutouts in a war camp re-creation.

The park's well-maintained trail system follow much of the original breastworks, with educational markers placed along the trails. The 1864 battle site has been restored, inviting exploration by young children. The swinging bridge leading to the site is a highlight also.

Designated a Wildlife Observation Area by Tennessee Wildlife Resources Agency, 1,650-acre Fort Pillow provides interpretive signs identifying certain species and their habitat. The popular Anderson-Tully hunting and fishing area is only 10 minutes to the north of the park's family camping area.

- The Visitor Center located near the entrance to Fort Pillow offers brochures and maps, as well as attractive nature and history displays, rest rooms, water, and a public telephone.

- The rustic campground has 40 sites available on a first-come, first-served basis. Up to 200 campers can use the group tent area; it is popular with such groups as Boy Scouts and Girls Scouts. Reservations required.

- Hikers can enjoy 15 miles of trails and a special camping area near the south end of the park.

- Picnickers can overlook Fort Pillow Lake while using the facilities provided (tables, grills, and water fountain, rest rooms and a playground). A pavilion may be rented for large groups.

- Fishing for bass, bream, crappie, and catfish in Fort Pillow Lake requires a Tennessee fishing license. Although there are no rental boats, a boat ramp is in place (gas motors prohibited).

- No hunting is allowed on park property.

Hours: Park: year-round, 8 a.m.-10 p.m. Interpretive Center and
              Office: 8 a.m.-4:30 p.m. Camper quiet time: 10 p.m.

Admission: FREE

Directions: Take U.S. Hwy. 51 north out of Memphis. Turn west onto
              State Hwy. 87. After going 17 miles and passing Fort
              Pillow Correctional Facility, turn north on State Hwy. 207,
              which leads to the park entrance. Road signs direct the
              18 miles from Hwy. 51 to the entrance.

JONESBORO, ARKANSAS

Northeast Arkansas's largest city, Jonesboro, is the home of Arkansas
State University, the Forum Civic Center, the world's largest rice mill,
historic homes, and Craighead Forest Park.

The Arkansas State University Museum, which began in 1936 as a glass
case of Native American artifacts, is a delightful point of interest for
families. Housed on the upper story of the Continuing Education Building
(just west of Dean B. Ellis Library), the compact and diversified gallery
space includes a "Toy Shop" filled with antique blocks, train cars, fire
engines, soldiers, and similar "play pretties" yellowed with age; "Mother
Goose on Parade" cases illustrating favorite nursery rhymes; several
furnished dollhouses of varying exterior architectural design; an actual
courthouse bell; Vietnamese traditional costumes and war-era uniforms;
life-like reproductions of an old dentist's office, one-room log cabin,
kitchen, stables, and more; a dug-out canoe; a large wooden loom and
other old manually operated machines and implements; cases of Native
American crafts and costumes from Apache, Sioux, Hopi, Choctaw, and
numerous other tribes; an archaeology display describing recovery techniques; a geology display; and various animal displays with such intriguing titles as "Moonlight Explorers," "Winged Hunters," and "Twilight
Browsers."

The self-guided tour begins through the double doors past the lobby gift shop, which features Native American crafts during the hours of 10 a.m.- 12 p.m. on Monday, Wednesday, and Friday, in addition to 1-4 p.m. on Sunday. The free museum itself is open 9 a.m.-4 p.m. Monday-Friday and 1-4 p.m. Saturday and Sunday, except during university holidays, when both the shop and gallery are closed. Guided tours may be arranged by appointment. Rest rooms, water fountain, and handicapped accessibility available. Call (501) 972-2074 for more information.

While in Jonesboro, you might want to visit city-owned Craighead Forest Park, only 3 1/2 miles south of town on scenic Crowley's Ridge. The 612-acre park, which contains an 80-acre lake, provides opportunities for fishing, boating, camping, and other activities. Park use is free. There are fees for pavilion use, camping and similar activities. The park is open 24 hours a day, seven days a week, but 10 p.m. marks the beginning of quiet time for campers. We are told that guests from all 50 states have enjoyed the facilities at Craighead Forest Park. For more information contact: Jonesboro Parks & Recreation Dept., P.O. Box 1845, Jonesboro, AR 72403. Phone (501) 933-4604.

Events of special interest to families in Jonesboro include the Fall Arts and Crafts Show and the Northeast Arkansas District Fair and Rodeo, both occurring in September.

The drive to Jonesboro begins in Memphis on I-40 west toward Little Rock. In Marion, Arkansas, take I-55 north; then turn onto Highway 63 north about 30 miles from Memphis. You might do some exploring on your own when passing through Trumann by turning left and seeing what the Trumann Museum has to offer. (Let us know if you think it should be included in the next edition of *Explore Memphis.*) When you reach Jonesboro (about 65 miles from Memphis), veer left to stay on Highway 63 when Highway 463 continues straight ahead. Exit right onto Caraway Road, and drive straight into the University of Arkansas campus. (The Continuing Education complex, which houses the museum, is in a cluster of buildings at the edge of the campus, to the left of Caraway Road.) To get to Craighead Forest Park, return to Highway 63, and continue west. Turn south onto Highway 141 (South Culberhouse), and travel 3 1/2 miles to the park.

MISSISSIPPI RIVER DELTA DRIVE:
CLARKSDALE, MISSISSIPPI and HELENA, ARKANSAS

The rich soils of the flat delta lands on either side of the lower Mississippi River produce bountiful agricultural crops and afford the highway traveler beautiful, rustic views of agrarian industry. An early autumn drive is sure to reveal such sights as huge harvesting machines filling up like giant popcorn poppers moving through the fluffy, snowy-white cotton fields; smokestacks pouring forth the evidence of the hard work under way at the numerous cotton gins dotting the landscape; gracefully terraced rice paddies pulsing in the breeze; and soybean fields bursting with lush greenness.

A double treat is the reward for a delta farmland tour that also crosses the mighty Mississippi River. We have mapped out one possible route for your day of experiencing the big river and its surrounding lands, with worthwhile stops along the way. (Our directions even lead you across the legendary Tallahatchie River Bridge.) You might want to be adventurous and map out your own course of travel.

From Memphis, take I-55 south to Highway 6 west. Travel past Batesville and Marks, observing the flattening of the land as you near the river and its centuries-old alluvial deposits.

At Clarksdale, Mississippi, go south on Highway 61, turn right onto de Soto Avenue, left on First Street, and left onto Delta Avenue. Delta Blues Museum, located in the main library building at 114 Delta Avenue, pays tribute through photographs, audio and video recordings, memorabilia, archives, and more to the blues heritage that sprouted up from its roots in the rich delta soil. The museum is open Monday-Friday from 9 a.m. until 5 p.m. year-round. Admission is free. For more information contact: Director, Carnegie Public Library, 114 Delta Avenue, P.O. Box 280, Clarksdale, MS 38614 or call (601/ 624-4461).

Now return to Highway 61 and head north toward Helena, Arkansas. Turn left at Rich onto Highway 49 west. As you must know by now, you'll get to cross the Mississippi River on your way to Arkansas. Your support across the muddy waters is an impressive multi-span, steel-truss bridge. Suddenly on the western banks of the river, turn right on Columbia toward historic Helena. Turn right again at Missouri Avenue, and follow it less than a mile to its ending in front of The Delta Cultural Center, housed in an old train depot right behind the town's levee and flood wall. This well-presented small museum is part of an ambitious six-phase project that will add new elements to the Helena landscape for the next several years. Opened in the fall of 1990, The Delta Cultural Center offers interesting exhibits on the river, the railroad, delta music, civil rights, historic packaging, the cotton industry, and more. Particularly appealing make-believe vehicles for children are the authentic-looking replica of a houseboat front porch and the restored train car. Excellent facilities, including a diversified gift shop and a wonderful brochure stand, are available. With free admission, the museum is open Monday-Saturday, 10 a.m.-5 p.m. and Sunday, noon-5 p.m.. For more information on the museum or projected additional phases of Helena's facelift, contact: The Delta Cultural Center, Visitors' Center, 95 Missouri St., Helena, AR 72342 or call (501/ 338-8919).

Other points of interest in Helena include the beautiful river view, several historic monuments, historic Cherry Street, The Old Almer Store, Estevan Hall, Phillips County Museum, and the nearby St. Francis National Forest (which offers picnicking, swimming, fishing, and camping). A walking tour brochure may be obtained at the Cultural Center. Festive annual events in Helena include the Antebellum Home Tours and the Music Festival (April-May), the Cherry Street Cruise (May); the Razorback Annual Fish Fry (June); the Halloween Parade and the King Biscuit Blues Festival (October); and the Arts and Crafts Show (November). For additional information contact Phillips County Chamber of Commerce, P.O. Box 447, Helena, AR 72342 or call (501/338-8327).

For a different view on the way back to Memphis, return to Highway 61 north, and follow it all the way home.

OXFORD, MISSISSIPPI

Oxford, Mississippi, a small college town about 80 miles from Memphis, offers the sophistication and cultural activity of a city many times its size along with the warmth and charm of a small town. The home of internationally acclaimed author William Faulkner, it is a magnet for writers, scholars, and students of literature from all around the world, especially during the Faulkner Conference held here each summer. A fashion mecca, as well, Oxford outfits college students and the regional best-dressed-list makers through its smart boutiques and Neilson's department store (the South's oldest, with a founding date of 1839).

We have outlined for you a typical sight-seeing day at Oxford, but let us warn you that the town is bursting with opportunities for pleasure that may distract you from your plans. If you get sidetracked by a workshop or festival or play, don't worry. Just return soon to complete your itinerary.

ROWAN OAK

Rowan Oak, Old Taylor Road, Oxford, Mississippi 38655 (601/234-3284). The home of Nobel Prize-winning novelist William Faulkner from 1930 until his death in 1962, Rowan Oak is set in a deeply wooded lot on Old Taylor Road near the University of Mississippi. The home was designated a National Historic Landmark in 1977 and is maintained by the University of Mississippi. Self-guided tours take visitors through both floors of the house, with Faulkner's office being perhaps the most interesting spot. The walls still bear the outline for the 1954 novel _A Fable,_ and his old typewriter still sits on a table near the window. The rambling grounds and out-buildings lend an air of serenity and peace to Rowan Oak.

On the day of our visit, William Faulkner's nephew stopped by to show some friends around the estate. The hilarious anecdotes he related would have made the trip worthwhile in themselves. Rowan Oak's associate curator assured us that the University staff would be happy to conduct tours for visitors on request, not necessarily as colorful as Mr. Faulkner's, but every bit as accurate historically.

- Fact sheets about the home available at the entrance.

- Free parking available on the residential streets around Rowan Oak.

- Handicapped accessibility appears very limited. Call (601/234-3284) for more information.

- No food, gift shop, rest rooms, or water available.

Hours: Tuesday-Saturday, 10 a.m.-noon, 2-4 p.m.; Sunday, 2-4 p.m. Closed Mondays and all major holidays.

Admission: FREE. (Donations to the fund for restoration and preservation of the site are gratefully accepted.)

Directions: From Memphis, take I-55 south to the Oxford exit (Highway 6 east). Take the ramp off Highway 6 to Old Taylor Road and turn left. Immediately after crossing the overpass, which is a part of this intersection, turn right onto an unmarked paved road. Continue less than a mile until the road makes a sharp right turn. Rowan Oak is to the left at this point. The driveway gate should be locked, but pedestrians can easily walk around it and down the cedar-lined driveway to the home.

UNIVERSITY MUSEUMS

University Museums, University Avenue, University, Mississippi 38677 (601) 232-7073. The Mary Buie Museum was established in 1939 by Kate Skipworth to fulfill the plans that she and her sister had made before Ms. Buie's death two years earlier. In 1976, 15 years after Ms. Skipworth's death, the Kate Skipworth Teaching Museum was constructed as an addition to the Mary Buie Museum. Together they make up the University Museums.

This facility houses such marvelously diverse exhibits as "Amazing, Ingenious, and Grotesque Things from our Collections" (an armadillo carapace basket, an Etruscan 4th century B.C. duck jug, a hair wreath, and a "thunder house," among other oddities); a physics collection dominated by a large 1854 orrery (working model of the solar system) and filled with fascinating instruments like the dynamometer and 1800 Atwood's Machine; a delightful collection of Southern folk art represented by such artists as Theora Hamblett, Luster Willis, and Mose Tolliver; a charmingly displayed collection of dolls manufactured from 1780 to 1920 in France, Germany, Scotland, the Netherlands, and other places near and far; a fully furnished, clearly inhabited Victorian room with an invitation for the viewer to "tell us your story of the room"; and much more. The David M. Robinson Collection of Greek and Roman antiquities is one of the finest in the United States.

- Excellent brochures on the museum and Oxford attractions are available.

- Plenty of free parking is available in the well-landscaped lot at the rear of the museum.

- The University's Center for the Study of Southern Culture is next door to the museum. It is open weekdays only.

- Family workshops take place on some weekends. Call (601/232-7205) for reservations.

- There is a small gift counter where items related to current exhibits may be purchased.

- The museum is fully handicapped accessible.

- Rest rooms and water fountain available.

- If this point in your tour is a good breaking time for lunch, we recommend either the picnic you brought to spread on the grounds or a quick drive to Square Books (east on University, left on S. Lamar Ave. to the town square—left-hand corner at Van

Buren Ave.), where you'll find delicious daily specials in the upstairs tea room (with outdoor balcony seating available) and a wonderful assortment of adults' and children's books all set in a cozy, intellectual atmosphere. Children will appreciate their special browsing nooks and the recycling IQ test in the dining area. (Square Books is open 9 a.m.-9 p.m. Monday-Thursday, 9 a.m.-10 p.m. Friday-Saturday, and noon-6 p.m. Sunday.)

Hours: University Museums is open Tuesday-Saturday, 10 a.m.-4 p.m.; Sunday, 1-4 p.m. Closed Mondays and all University holidays.

Admission: FREE. (Donations gratefully accepted.)

Directions: From Rowan Oak, take Taylor Road north to University Avenue. Turn right, then right again at 5th Street.

UNIVERSITY CAMPUS BUILDINGS

Drive back along University Avenue to the campus. Park at the first available space near University Loop, and enjoy a leisurely stroll around the grove and along the streets. Look especially for the following important buildings:

Lyceum—built in 1848, the only survivor of the original campus of the first public institution of higher education in Mississippi, the site of a hospital during the Civil War.

Ventress Hall—built in 1889 as a library, later used for law classes (then geology, now art), distinguished by its Gothic architecture and stained-glass panels on back wall commemorating the mustering of the University Greys in the Civil War.

Fulton Chapel—built in 1927 as a student chapel, now the site of theatrical productions, concerts, and other programs.

Blues Archive—located in room 340 of Farley Hall, the world's most extensive collection of blues recordings and related materials (open 8:30 a.m.-5 p.m. Monday-Friday).

Old Chapel—the "Y" building, dating from 1853.

J.D. Williams Library—housing numerous manuscript collections, the William Faulkner Collection, and other "Mississippiana."

TUPELO, MISSISSIPPI

Although Tupelo is slightly farther than our other day trips in this chapter (approximately 100 miles from Memphis), we felt that visitors to Memphis as well as natives feel a kinship with this rapidly growing southern city. One of Memphis's most illustrious "sons," Elvis Presley, was born in Tupelo on January 8, 1935, and hundreds of people make the pilgrimage to his birthplace each year.

To get to Tupelo, take Highway 78 south. On the way you'll notice the turnoff for Highway 7 around Holly Springs. If you have time, you might want to take this short side step on your way to Tupelo. Eight miles south down Highway 7 is the **Wall Doxey State Park.** Overlooking the spring-fed waters of its 60-acre lake is a stately lodge. Plenty of picnic spots are dotted throughout the park, and canoeing, pedal boating, and fishing are popular activities.

Back on Highway 78, the road will take you all the way to Tupelo. Your first stop in Tupelo might be the Tupelo Convention and Visitors Bureau, (601) 841-6521. Located on N. Gloster Street, the Bureau has maps, brochures, and information to make your visit to the area enjoyable. We've listed a few of our suggestions to get you started on your adventure.

ELVIS PRESLEY BIRTHPLACE

Elvis Presley Birthplace, 306 Elvis Presley Drive, Tupelo (601/841-1245). Visit the two-room frame house where the King of Rock 'n Roll was born. A Memorial Chapel, financed completely by donations from Elvis's fans and friends, is on the property. Other facilities include a gift shop, Youth Center, park, and playground. A brochure is available, directing interested visitors on a four-mile driving tour, hitting such spots as the Tupelo hardware store where Elvis bought his first guitar and two of the schools Elvis attended as a youth.

Center Hours: Monday-Saturday (May through September), 9 a.m.-5:30 p.m.; Monday-Saturday (October-April), 9 a.m.-5 p.m.; Sunday, 1-5 p.m. year-round.

Admission: Adults, $1; children (under 12), 50 cents.

TUPELO CITY MUSEUM

Tupelo City Museum, Ballard Park just off Highway 6 west, Tupelo (601/841-6438). Fascinating exhibits, many of interest to children, await you at this charming museum. Indian artifacts and Civil War displays will be a favorite for the explorers in your group. The NASA space hangar features the latest in space technology, with many hands-on displays that let children's imaginations carry them off into the wild blue yonder. A replica of an old schoolroom and an unusual collection of antique hats take children on a delightful trip back in history.

Hours: Tuesday-Friday, 10 a.m.-4 p.m.; Saturday-Sunday, 1-5 p.m.

Admission: FREE.

MISSISSIPPI MUSEUM OF ART

Mississippi Museum of Art, 211 West Main Street, Tupelo (601) 844-2787. Traveling exhibits from all over the country are shown at this typical small-city museum. You might want to stop while on your way at the fish hatchery to check out the display.

Hours: Tuesday-Saturday, 10 a.m.-5 p.m.; Sunday, 1-5 p.m.

Admission: FREE.

PVT. JOHN M. ALLEN NATIONAL FISH HATCHERY

Pvt. John M. Allen National Fish Hatchery, 111 East Elizabeth Street, Tupelo (601/842-1341). If you've never visited a fish hatchery, this surely should be your first. Hatching millions of fish each year, the hatchery offers the added treasure of its beautiful location. The Tupelo Garden Club has done a splendid job of restoring the 1903 Victorian house on the property. Free tours are available by contacting the Convention and Visitors Bureau.

NATIONAL BATTLEFIELD SITES

Brice's Crossroads. This area was the scene of a significant Confederate victory over Union forces in June, 1864. Military experts agree that this engagement was the hardest kind of fighting and produced a brilliant victory for the gray coats. The park consists of only a small piece of land, but from it much of the field of action is within view. Located 15 miles north of Tupelo off U.S. Highway 45.

Battle of Tupelo. Located within the city limits of Tupelo, this site is near the place where the Confederate line was formed to attack the Union position. A major conflict between the North and South was fought here in 1864. Located on West Main Street.

NATCHEZ TRACE PARKWAY

Connecting the southwestern Mississippi city of Natchez with Nashville, Tennessee, is the Natchez Trace Parkway. Headquarters for this historic route is in Tupelo. Stop at the Natchez Trace Visitors Center, (601) 842-

1572, five miles north of Tupelo, and watch the 12-minute orientation film. The Center has a unique hands-on display for kids, allowing them to enjoy toys from the 1800s.

WHITEVILLE, TENNESSEE

ANDERSON FRUIT FARMS FARM MARKET

Anderson Fruit Farms Farm Market, Highway 64, Route 1, Box 6A, Whiteville, Tennessee 38075 (1-254-9530). At Anderson orchards, a Whiteville fixture for several decades, peaches, pears, plums, and nectarines are grown. Shoppers are invited to select their produce right off the trees from around Labor Day until the harvest is completed. Particularly appealing on the day of our visit to the roadside stand were the Keiffer preserving pears and a wide variety of apples—Melrose, Paducah, Ozark Gold, Jonathan, Winesap, and of course Red and Golden Delicious.

Inside the enclosed market, we found fresh-squeezed and bottled, pasteurized apple cider along with a slightly-faded, but still interesting photo display of the cider-making process. Culinary delights caught our attention at every turn as we spied hanging sugar-cured hams, fresh sweet potatoes, new molasses, and jars of blackberry jam, hot chow chow, and green tomato relish. Apple recipe booklets add a final bit of interest to this down-home fruit market.

BÄCKERMANN'S MENNONITE BAKERY

Bäckermann's Mennonite Bakery, Highway 64, Route 1, Whiteville, Tennessee 38075 (1-254-8473). The seductive fragrances of cinnamon and yeast were the first greeting we sensed as we entered this family-owned and -operated bakery in Whiteville, Tennessee, just next door to

Anderson's Fruit Market. Next we noticed the instrumental version of "Blessed Assurance" playing quietly and soothingly, yes nostalgically, on the sound system. Finally, with our ears and noses transported back in time, we began our journey of visual stimulation.

One big refrigerated wall is laden with fresh-baked pies—pecan, apple, cherry, blackberry, and even shoo fly—and cheeses from Ohio—big chunks of Colby, farmer's, and baby Swiss. On stacked shelves are laid out packages of bay leaves, whole coriander, ground ginger, and other fresh spices, alongside such "dry goods" as cotton hankies, hair nets, zippers, cotton socks, and spools of thread. Fireballs, smarties, yogurt raisins, old-fashioned horehound, and peppermint are a few of the bagged candies tempting a sweet tooth. Country delicacies such as new crop sorghum molasses, honey, and apple butter are interspersed with gourds, Indian corn, dried fruit, and greeting cards.

The immaculate kitchen area is clearly visible from the browsing area of the bakery. Large commercial ovens work to turn out the rolls and other baked products that have been mixed and kneaded and shaped on the long work table. The sole worker on the day of our visit was busy slathering a rich, tan-colored icing on hot pans of sweet rolls.

After gathering up and paying for our delicious pies, breads, and cookies, we asked about the bakery and its background. We found out that in German a "bäckermann" is a baker, hence the descriptive name (which we had assumed incorrectly to be the family name). The Mennonite owners quietly demonstrate their religious beliefs through brief testimonials on the labels of the packaged goods, rather than hard-sell proselytizing, and questions are answered politely and succinctly.

For a perfect day's outing, we suggest a drive out Highway 64 to Anderson's and Bäckermann's—about 15 miles east of Somerville, or 41 miles east of Memphis. (As the helpful person told us in our telephone inquiry about the location, "If you get to Whiteville, you've gone too far.") Take an empty picnic basket with you, and fill it at the market and bakery with fresh-baked breads and cookies, a slab of your favorite cheese, a jar of jam, and a bag of fresh fruit. Grab a jug of apple cider, head back toward Memphis, and stop at **Eads Galleries** (see Eads listing in Chapter 3) for a lovely picnic spread on the quilt you've brought along for this purpose. (Eads, which is closed the first few months of the year, is open only on weekends the rest of the year, so if you plan your outing on a weekday, you'll have to make arrangements beforehand to see the artwork at Eads.) If you've chosen a Tuesday (May-October) for your day-trip, you may even have time for a stop at **Davies Plantation** (see listing in Chapter 3) for a charming dose of Shelby County history and lore.

Hours: Anderson's is open from 9 a.m. to 5 p.m. year-round (with an additional hour or two of daily business in the spring and summer). Bäckermann's is open 7 a.m.-5:30 p.m. Tuesday-Saturday and 11 a.m.-5 p.m. Mondays.

Admission: Free admission to the bakery and fruit market.

Directions: From Memphis take I-40 toward Nashville. Get off at Exit #18 (Highway 64) toward Somerville. Continue driving east (right turn at the exit). Enjoy passing through picturesque Somerville and the surrounding countryside covered with barns, cattle, horses, and cotton fields. Just past a silo on the right-hand side of the highway—and before the town of Whiteville—is Bäckermann's Mennonite Bakery; then less than a mile further on down the road is Anderson Fruit Farms Farm Market, also on the right.

OTHER PLACES TO EXPLORE (AND STARTING POINTS)

Bolivar, Tennessee (Historic homes and buildings)

Corinth, Mississippi (Northeast Mississippi Museum)

Earle, Arkansas (Crittenden County Museum)

Germantown, Tennessee (Germantown Festival)

Greenwood, Mississippi (Cottonlandia Museum)

Hernando, Mississippi (The McIngvale Clock Museum and Arkabutla Lake)

Holly Springs, Mississippi (Kate Freeman Clark Art Gallery and Spring Pilgrimage Home Tour)

Humboldt, Tennessee (Strawberry Festival in May)

Jackson, Tennessee (Casey Jones Home Railroad Museum)

Milan, Tennessee (West Tennessee Agricultural Museum)

Pickwick Dam, Tennessee (Pickwick Landing State Resort Park)

Ripley, Mississippi (First Monday Trade Day)

Sardis, Mississippi (Sardis Lake)

Scott, Arkansas (Plantation Agriculture Museum and nearby Toltec Mounds Archaeological State Park)

Senatobia, Mississippi (Tate County Heritage Museum)

Shiloh, Tennessee (Shiloh National Military Park)

Stuttgart, Arkansas (Stuttgart Agricultural Museum)

Tiptonville, Tennessee (Reelfoot Lake State Resort Park)

Trenton, Tennessee (Teapot Festival in May—(901/855-0973)

West Memphis, Arkansas (Delta Farm Tours)

Wilson, Arkansas (Hampson Museum State Park)

Wynne, Arkansas (Village Creek State Park)

8. Resources

SPECIAL ASSISTANCE TELEPHONE NUMBERS

Ambulance, Fire, Police 911
AIDS Information and Testing—Shelby Co. Health 576-7714
Al-Anon/Al-A-Teen 766-9733
Alcohol and Drug Council 274-0056
Alcoholics Anonymous 454-1414
Alliance for the Blind & Visually Impaired............................454-1244
American Red Cross—Memphis 726-1690
Autism Society of America—Memphis.....................................360-9407
Birth Certificates 576-7605
Boys' Town—Memphis 386-2040
Cancer Society, American—Memphis & Shelby Co. 382-9500
Cerebral Palsy United—Mid-South Office 323-0190
Child Abuse Hotline—Dept. of Human Services.......................543-7120
Child Abuse Squad—Memphis Police Department....................576-5220
Child Sexual Abuse Council 327-0893
Clinic Info.—Shelby Co. Health Dept 576-7551
Community Services—Shelby County 576-4274
Crippled Children's Service 543-6848
Crisis Center 274-7477
Cystic Fibrosis Foundation 682-8373
Deaf Services (Interpreting and other services)
    Voice 577-3783
    TDD 577-3784
Easter Seals..368-0532
Epilepsy Foundation 452-7144
Family Service of Memphis (counseling) 324-3637
Hearing Impaired Services—Shelby County 576-4584
Heart Association, American—of Tennessee 526-4616
Hemophilia Foundation 458-6727
Homework Hotline—Memphis City Schools............................325-5050
Jewish Family Services (counseling) 767-8511
Juvenile Court (counseling for unruly children) 528-8497
La Leche League 452-3383
LeBonheur Children's Medical Center....................................522-3000

LINC Information & Referral 725-8895
Make-A-Wish Foundation® 272-9474
March of Dimes 682-8483
Mayor's Action Center—Memphis 576-6500
Mayor's Citizens Assistance—Shelby County 576-4584
Mayor's Human Services Bureau—Memphis 576-6503
Memphis Area Cooperative Services (goods, training) 272-3700
Memphis City Schools 454-5200
Memphis Oral School for the Deaf 577-8490
Memphis Sexual Assault Resource Center 528-2161
MIFA (Memphis Inter-Faith Association) 527-0208
Missing Children Hotline .... (800) 843-5678
National Conference of Christians & Jews 327-0010
Nutrition Consultant—Shelby Co. Health Dept 576-7780
Organ Transplant Fund 684-1697
Parenting & Race Relations—Memphis City Schools 775-7266
Parenting Center of Memphis 452-3830
Parents Without Partners 458-9643
Physicians Referral Services
    Baptist Memorial Hospital 362-8677
    LeBonheur Children's Medical Center...............................522-3079
    Memphis/Shelby Co. Medical Society 761-0200
    Methodist Med Search 726-8686
    St. Francis Hospital 765-1811
    St. Joseph Hospital 576-8723
Poison Control Center (Southern) 528-6048
Prenatal Services 576-7646
Public Information—Memphis City Schools 325-5628
Runaway Hotline .... (800) 231-6946
St. Jude Children's Research Hospital 522-0306
Shelby County Schools 325-7900
Sickle Cell Council 276-7339
Special Education—Memphis City Schools 325-5600
Special Education—Shelby County 373-2603
Toy Safety Hotline .... (800) 638-2772
Tuberculosis Control—Shelby County Health Dept. 576-3616
United Way 578-6600
Wife Abuse Services—YWCA 458-1661

YMCA 458-3580
Youth Service in Memphis (programs for at-risk youth) 452-5600

CONVENTION AND VISITOR'S BUREAUS

ARKANSAS WELCOME CENTER

From Memphis take I-40 west across the Hernando de Soto Bridge. The welcome center is one mile west of Airport Road. (501) 735-3637.

Lots of helpful, up-to-date brochures are available. Attractive arts and crafts displays include corn-shuck doll, applehead dolls, wood carvings, pottery, and a mini-bale of cotton. Picnic tables, vending machines, water, rest rooms, and maps also available.

MISSISSIPPI WELCOME CENTER

From Memphis take I-55 south. The welcome center is one mile south of the Hernando exit. (601) 429-9969.

The colonial-style building sits on a well-landscaped lot. In addition to excellent brochures, the welcome center offers picnic tables, rest rooms, water, maps, and complimentary beverages. Local crafts displayed include pewter, pottery, jewelry, and sand sculptures.

TENNESSEE WELCOME CENTER

From the Mississippi Welcome Center, return north on I-55. The Tennessee station is one mile north of the Shelby Drive exit. (901) 345-5956.

You'll notice the modern pipe sculpture outside the center. The geometrically placed posts of graduated heights create a three-dimensional design that alternates between orange, white, and blue, depending on the angle from which the outdoor sculpture is viewed. A world of brochures is available, in addition to picnic tables, vending machines, rest rooms, water, maps, and a dog walk.

COLLIERVILLE CHAMBER OF COMMERCE
125 N. Rowlett • 853-1949

GERMANTOWN CHAMBER OF COMMERCE
Depot Square Park
Germantown Rd. South • 755-1200

MEMPHIS AREA CHAMBER OF COMMERCE
22 N. Front • 575-3500

MEMPHIS CITY BEAUTIFUL COMMISSION
664 Adams Avenue • 528-2718

MEMPHIS COMMUNITY CALENDAR
1850 Peabody Ave. • 725-8895

MEMPHIS CONVENTION AND VISITORS BUREAU
50 N. Front Street • 576-8181

MEMPHIS CONVENTION CENTER
255 N. Main • 576-1200

MEMPHIS VISITOR INFORMATION CENTER
340 Beale Street • 526-4880

**WEST MEMPHIS, ARKANSAS, ADVERTISING
AND PROMOTION COMMISSION**
P.O. Box 1728
W. Memphis, AR 72303 • (501) 735-2720

PUBLICATIONS

MEMPHIS NEWSPAPERS

The Commercial Appeal, Memphis Publishing Company, 495 Union Avenue, Memphis, TN 38103 (529-2345). Memphis's daily newspaper offers several features especially aimed at children. "The Kids Appeal" page, which comes out each Monday, features games, trivia, children's poetry and artwork, and educational pieces. Children's books are reviewed regularly in the Sunday book section. Weekly and daily calendars of local events include children's listings. Daily edition, 50 cents; Sunday edition, $1.50. Available at local stores and mobile newsstands. Subscription rate is $13.95 per month.

The Daily News, 193 Jefferson, Memphis, TN (523-1561).

The Memphis Business Journal, 88 Union Center, Suite 102, Memphis, TN 38103 (523-0437). This weekly newspaper rivals the daily newspaper in providing in-depth looks at major current news stories in the area. It also offers excellent reviews of plays, movies, and other family entertainment.

The Memphis Flyer, 460 Tennessee Street, P.O. Box 687, Memphis, TN 38103 (521-9000). This tabloid is a spin-off from the parent company of *Memphis* magazine. Published weekly, it is available FREE at local newsstands, restaurants, etc. Although most of the newspaper is adult-oriented, it does include useful calendars and schedules of many family-appropriate activities.

Memphis Parent, Memphis Parent, Inc., MIFA, 910 Vance, Memphis, TN 38107 (527-0208). "For families with children under 14 years old." Chock-full of excellent illustrated articles about child development, travel, books, family activities, volunteer projects, and more. Published bi-monthly.

FREE. Available at libraries and public book stands. (A one year subscription is $6.)

Tri-State Defender, 24 E. Calhoun, Memphis, TN (523-1818).

COMMUNITY NEWSPAPERS

The Collierville Independent, 215 Center St., Collierville, TN (853-7060).

The Evening Times, 111 E. Bond West Memphis, Arkansas (735-1010).

The Express, 2874 Shelby Street, Bartlett, TN (388-1500).

Germantown News, 7545 North Street, Germantown, TN (754-0337).

Millington Star, 5107 Easley, Millington, TN (872-2286).

Shelby Sun Times, 7508 Capitol, Germantown, TN (755-7386).

Southaven Press, 1800 State Line Road East, Southaven, MS (393-3840).

NEIGHBORHOOD NEWSPAPERS
(distributed FREE in restaurants, libraries, newsstands, etc.)

Chamber Works, Collierville Chamber of Commerce, Depot Town Square, Collierville, TN 38017 (853-1949).

Downtown Update, Center City Commission, 22 N. Front, Suite 680, Memphis, TN 38103 (526-6840). Monthly pamphlet listing current events.

The Downtowner, P.O. Box 3367, Memphis, TN 38173 (525-7118). Published monthly.

The LampLighter, 619 N. Seventh Street, Memphis, TN 38107-3721 (526-6627). Monthly news of the Cooper-Young Community. Center for Neighborhoods.

Memphis Neighborhoods, The Center for Neighborhoods, 619 N. Seventh St., Memphis, TN 38107 (526-6627).

─────── **AGENCY/SPECIAL INTEREST NEWSLETTERS** ───────
(distributed FREE at the site of origination and some other public places):

The Hebrew Watchman, 4646 Poplar, Suite 232, Memphis, TN (763-2215).

Memphis Health Care News, 88 Union Center, Suite 200, Memphis, TN (526-2007).

Memphis Shoppers Guide, 622 S. Highland, Memphis, TN (458-8030).

Mid-South Hunting and Fishing News, 3251 Poplar, Memphis, TN (458-7899).

Parent Connections, Parenting Center of Memphis, 499 Patterson, Memphis, TN 38111 (452-3830). Published quarterly. One-year subscription available for $10 donation. Also available FREE in the public library and various other public locations.

Real Estate News, 3534 Park ,Memphis, TN (458-1447).

Travelhost, P.O. Box 41162, Memphis, TN (725-9283).

──────────────── **BOOKS** ────────────────

A Child's Guide to Memphis, Morgan Press (1991). This coloring book has drawings of 21 significant Memphis landmarks. Useful resources are listed in the back. Created by Renee P. Cooley and illustrated by James A. Caldwell, the $3.95 book can be found at major local book stores.

City on the Bluff: History and Heritage of Memphis, The Friends of Memphis and Shelby County Libraries. This excellent little Memphis history book is delightfully illustrated by Memphis children. It is sold at the check-out desk of the main library on Peabody for $9.95.

Me, Myself 'n Memphis: A Book of Activities for Children, WonderWords, P.O. Box 12392, Memphis, TN 38182-0392. Our own (Debbie and Marci's) book of activities to complete at eight of the locations we have described for you here. $7.95. Available at major Memphis bookstores. 1991.

The Peabody Ducks, Duck Tail Productions, P.O. Box 11159, Memphis, TN 38111. Detailing one of Memphis's unique attractions, this little keepsake book offers 23 pages of colorful drawings and amusing text. Created by Jean J. Garbarini, written by Martha L. Garrety, and illustrated by Phyllis Bailey (1982). Available at major local bookstores.

BOOKLETS

Surviving Summer and _Getting Ready for Summer._ Two excellent resources for parents trying to ensure a worthwhile, productive summer for their children. Guides list recreation, day camps, sports, service opportunities, and more. Available at the main library on Peabody Avenue. 725-8895.

MAGAZINES

Memphis, MM Corporation, 460 Tennessee Street, Memphis, TN 38103 (521-9000). This high-gloss, fancy-looking magazine is really a down-home monthly look at Memphis—where we are, where we've been, where we're going. In addition to its many timely articles on topics of interest to local parents, it offers calendars of events, lists of restaurants and entertainment, and other regular features of great use to families as resources. $1.95 per copy. Available at all local newsstands or by subscription (about $15 per year).

TELEPHONE SERVICES

Dial An' Smile
278-2370

J. C. Levy, the legendary, long-time operator of the children's rides at the Memphis Zoo, writes and records dear little corny, animal-related poems and jokes that are sure to delight young children. He ends his message with a plug for the zoo.

FUNLINE
529-2500 (outside Memphis, call 800-444-6397, Ext. 2500)

Running 24 hours a day, seven days a week is an educational suggestion for parents to use in helping their preschool and elementary-aged children develop reading skills. Sponsored by *The Commercial Appeal's* education department, the telephone messages are changed each Wednesday.

Time of Day Service
526-5261

Recorded telephone message gives accurate time of day and current temperature along with a brief commercial advertisement. Children enjoy verifying the settings on all the clocks in the house, especially when they are just learning how to tell time.

TOP 20 PLACES TO GO

Adventure River
Agricenter International
Audubon Park
The Children's Museum of Memphis
Chucalissa Archaeological Museum
Dixon Gallery and Gardens

Graceland
Historic Beale Street
Libertyland
Lichterman Nature Center
Meeman-Shelby State Park
Memphis Botanic Garden
Memphis Brooks Museum of Art
Memphis Pink Palace Museum
Memphis Queen Line
Memphis Zoo and Aquarium/Overton Park
Mississippi River/Mud Island
National Civil Rights Museum
The Pyramid
Victorian Village

FREE ACTIVITIES FOR FAMILIES

Agricenter International
Animal Shelters and Humane Society
Art Galleries
Audubon Park
Bookstores
Center for Southern Folklore
Chickasaw Garden Lake
City Hall
Cordova Cellars
Crystal Shrine Grotto—Memorial Park
Danny Thomas/ALSAC Pavilion
Dixon Gallery and Gardens*
Downtown Christmas Tree Lighting
Downtown Park Tour
EARTH Complex
Elmwood Cemetery
Farmer's Markets
Goodwin's Greenhouses
Historic Beale Street

Hotel Hopping
Laurel Hill Vineyards
Magevney House
Meeman-Shelby State Park
Memphis Botanic Garden*
Memphis Brooks Museum of Art*
Memphis International Airport
Memphis Police Museum
Memphis Zoo*
Mississippi River
National Civil Rights Museum*
The National Ornamental Metal Museum*
Nurseries
Overton Park
Overton Square
Parades
The Peabody
Pet Stores
Playgrounds
Public Libraries
A. Schwab
Shelby County Courthouse
Shelby Farms
Shopping Malls
T.O. Fuller State Park
Tours of the Working World
Toy Stores
U.S. Post Office—Front Street Station
Victorian Village Walking Tour

*During limited hours these attractions are free to the public.

BIRTHDAY PARTY IDEAS

Adventure River
Audubon Park

Bowling
Chickasaw Gardens Lake
The Children's Museum of Memphis
Children's Theatre
Chucalissa Archaeological Museum
Downtown Park Tour
Eads Gallery
Elmwood Cemetery (Tombstone Rubbings)
Gymnastic Centers
Happy Times Farm
Historic Beale Street
Ice Skating
Libertyland
Lichterman Nature Center
Malibu Grand Prix
Maywood Beach
Meeman-Shelby State Park
Memphis Botanic Garden
Memphis Chicks Baseball Game
Memphis Zoo and Aquarium
Miniature Golf
Mud Island
National Ornamental Metal Museum
Overton Park
The Peabody
Playgrounds
Pony Rides
Puppet Shows
Roller Skating
Shelby Farms
Spacewalk's Fun-Plex
Story Times—Library and Bookstores
Swimming
T.O. Fuller State Park
Tours of the Working World
U.S.A. Baseball Game

RAINY WEATHER IDEAS

Animal Shelters and Humane Society
Art Galleries
Bookstores
Bowling
Center for Southern Folklore
The Children's Museum of Memphis
Children's Theatre
City Hall
Danny Thomas/ALSAC Pavilion
Dixon Gallery
Graceland
Gymnastic Centers
Hardware Stores
Hobby Shows, Flea Markets, Collector Fairs
Hobby Stores
Hotel Hopping
Ice Skating
Magevney House
Mallory-Neely House
Memphis Brooks Museum of Art
Memphis College of Art
Memphis Music and Blues Museum
Memphis Pink Palace Museum
Memphis Police Museum
Memphis State University Museum
National Bird Dog Museum
National Civil Rights Museum
The Peabody
Pet Stores
Public Libraries
Roller Skating
A. Schwab
Shelby County Courthouse
Shopping Malls

Spacewalk's Fun-Plex
Sun Record Studio
Tennis—Indoor
Tours of the Working World
Toy Stores
Woodruff-Fontaine House

COLLEGES AND UNIVERSITIES

Memphis offers a variety of educational opportunities through its colleges and universities—from two-year community colleges to specialized professional schools. This is a listing of the major higher education institutions in Memphis.

Christian Brothers University, 650 East Parkway (722-0200) Emphasizes engineering, telecommunications, and science.

LeMoyne-Owen College, 807 Walker (774-9090). One of the oldest African-American colleges in the U.S.

Memphis College of Art, Overton Park (726-4085). A private, four-year college offering the B.F.A. degree.

Memphis State University, Central Avenue (678-2000). Comprising six undergraduate colleges, a graduate school, a nursing school, and a law school, MSU is the largest institution of higher education in Memphis. Memphis State also offers an incredible assortment of children's and parents' courses through its continuing education department—such classes as waterbabies, preschool gymnastics, ice skating, karate, guitar, kindermusik, ballet, art experiences, preparation for ACT and SAT, and many, many more.

Rhodes College, 2000 North Parkway (274-1800). Frequently cited as one of the top liberal arts colleges in the U.S.

Shelby State Community College, 737 Union Avenue (528-6700).

Offers certificates, associate degrees, and pre-baccalaureate degrees on completion of its two-year programs.

Southern College of Optometry, 1245 Madison Avenue (722-3200). Offers bachelor of science and doctor of optometry degrees and operates clinics for student training.

State Technical Institute at Memphis, 5983 Macon Cove (377-4111). Tennessee's largest two-year college, State Tech offers associate degrees in three major areas of study: business, engineering, and computer science.

The University of Tennessee, Memphis, 800 Madison (528-5500). An academic health center and biomedical research center.

9. Index

Symbols

A

B

C

D

E

J

K

L

M